MW00948134

NIA
BER

TON

ORK
TEE
IBER

December 17, 2024

Dear Colleague:

In January 2023, Speaker Kevin McCarthy asked me to take on a new and challenging task; investigating the security failures at the Capitol on January 6, 2021, as well as the actions, investigation, and subsequent report of the Pelosi-appointed Select Committee on January 6.

I accepted this assignment on two conditions; that I have the autonomy and resources needed to effectively pursue the facts without political bias or outside influence, and that I have the authority to report whatever we find to the American people. McCarthy assured me that I would be given what I needed to conduct a real investigation and proper oversight. Since that day, I have taken this responsibility very seriously; and over the past two years, my team and I have aggressively pursued the truth and made public the evidence as we have uncovered the facts.

Over the past twenty-four months of this investigation, my subcommittee staff have faced incredible obstacles in pursuit of the truth; missing and deleted documents, hidden evidence, unaccounted for video footage, and uncooperative bureaucrats. At one point, the work of the subcommittee was completely halted due to the removal of Kevin McCarthy as Speaker, and subsequently faced internal efforts to derail the investigation. However, our team persevered through the delays; and, when Mike Johnson took the gavel as Speaker of the House, he allocated even more resources to our investigation and committed to more transparency for the American people.

Over the course of the 118th Congress, the Subcommittee on Oversight has worked many late nights and numerous weekends in their relentless pursuit of truth. We interviewed hundreds of witnesses, scoured over millions of pages of documents, analyzed thousands of hours of surveillance videos, listened to hundreds of hours of radio communications, and conducted hearings. I appreciate my team's commitment to the mission, as well as their unwavering dedication to this vitally important cause. Every member and staff member of this subcommittee deserves the gratitude of those whose reputations have been restored, as well as those who have been exonerated by the evidence they have exposed. From the D.C. National Guard, who were maligned by false reports from the Pentagon to the former Chief of Capitol Police, Steven Sund, who unfairly shouldered the bulk of the blame for the security failures of that day, many have had a level of hope restored, due to the work of this subcommittee.

This report reveals that there was not just one single cause for what happened at the U.S. Capitol on January 6; but it was a series of intelligence, security, and leadership failures at several levels and numerous entities. Even amid multiple failures, there were two common elements that significantly contributed to the security issues: an excessive amount of political influence on critical decisions, and a greater concern over the optics than for protecting life and property. But as with many government scandals, the cover up of evidence exacerbated our efforts to find the facts and expose the truth; but our team never gave up.

During the ten years that I have served in Congress, I have had many memorable experiences. I have sat in the Oval Office and the Cabinet Room at the White House negotiating legislation with the President, flown on Air Force One, and traveled overseas to meet with foreign heads of state. However, I can unequivocally say that, above all of that, the work we have accomplished over the past two years on this subcommittee has given me a greater sense of accomplishment, and a clarity in my purpose for being in Congress.

While there is still much more to be investigated, Congress must take what we have learned thus far and begin the arduous task of making reforms within both the Legislative and Executive Branches to ensure this level of security failure can never happen again.

The American people deserve a government they can trust and be proud of. Unfortunately, the failures, coverups and false accusations in the aftermath of January 6 have only increased the people's distrust of Washington D.C. I hope the work of this subcommittee will help restore a level of hope in our government; but, until we hold accountable those responsible, and reform our institutions, we will not fully regain trust.

Americans expect and deserve a government that is small in size, limited in scope, and fully accountable to the people, as our Founders intended. The actions of some elected officials and certain government bureaucrats in the aftermath of January 6, 2021, are evidence of how we have ventured far away from those basic principles of our constitutional republic. Transparency, accountability, and equal application of the law are the only solutions to return our nation to one that is free, safe and full of opportunity. I sincerely pray that this report is just the beginning of an era of restoring our federal government to the basic principles of transparency and accountability.

God Bless,

Barry Loudermilk
Chairman
Subcommittee on Oversight
Committee on House Administration

CONTENTS

INTRODUCTION

The Committee on House Administration Subcommittee on Oversight, Chaired by Congressman Barry Loudermilk (GA-11), has spent the past two years of the 118th Congress investigating the security failures of January 6, 2021, which House Democrats failed to investigate in their 117th Congress "Select Committee to Investigate the January 6th Attack on the United States Capitol" ("Select Committee.")

The purpose of this investigation was to identify and review the numerous security failures on and leading up to January 6, 2021, and to review the creation, operation, and results of Speaker Nancy Pelosi's Select Committee.

Speaker Pelosi and House Democrats spent millions of taxpayer dollars on their politically motivated Select Committee yet failed to accurately, and in a bipartisan manner, investigate the security failures of that day. Instead, the members of the Select Committee were laser-focused on their effort to promote their false, pre-determined narrative that President Trump was personally responsible for the breach of the Capitol on January 6 and should therefore be held accountable, by any means necessary.

Throughout its nearly two years of work, the Select Committee presented uncorroborated, cherry-picked, and, at times, false evidence that fit its narrative. The Select Committee did not attempt to hide its bias, and, in fact, memorialized its own failures and prejudice when it published its Final Report in December 2022. A review of the nearly one-thousand-page report reveals Speaker Pelosi's multimillion-dollar Select Committee was a political weapon with a singular focus to deceive the public into blaming President Trump for the violence on January 6 and to tarnish the legacy of his first Presidency.

The Select Committee wholeheartedly failed to address the security failures on January 6, 2021, and failed to archive significant portions of the evidence it collected and used to formulate its conclusions. As a result, the Capitol is no safer today than it was at the creation of the Select Committee. The mission of Chairman Loudermilk's Subcommittee this Congress was to identify the truth for the American public and conduct the investigation originally tasked to the Select Committee.

To provide truth, full transparency, and fulfill our commitment to the American people, we spent this past Congress investigating why the Capitol was ill-prepared and what security changes are needed to ensure adequate protection for Members of Congress, the thousands of staff who work in the Capitol complex, and the millions of people who visit the site each year.

Our goal for the 118th Congress was not to rewrite the events of January 6 nor to promote a political narrative. It is the firm belief of the Subcommittee that it is Congress's duty to provide full transparency to the American people so they can draw their own conclusions based on all the information available, not just the information that supports one perspective.

This report summarizes the past two years of investigation by the Subcommittee and findings based on nonpartisan evidence, firsthand accounts of events, and thorough comparisons of official records, hearings, and letters at the direction of Chairman Barry Loudermilk.

Chairman Loudermilk and the Committee on House Administration Oversight Subcommittee ("Subcommittee") has jurisdiction over the records created by former Speaker Nancy Pelosi's partisan January 6 Select Committee. Unfortunately, a substantial portion of those records were deleted or otherwise withheld from the Subcommittee. Chairman Loudermilk has worked tirelessly to retrieve the deliberately lost evidence and complete the picture of the events of January 6, regardless of politics or optics. The truth will prevail.

Rule 10 of the House Rules of the 118th Congress state that the Committee on House Administration ("Committee") has jurisdiction over the "administration of the House Office Buildings and of the House wing of the Capitol."[1] This includes oversight of the United States Capitol Police ("USCP") and the security of the Capitol complex.[2]

Chairman Loudermilk and the Subcommittee are charged with "the records of the [January 6] Select Committee."[3] Specifically, at the start of the 118th Congress, the resolution adopting the Rules of the House reiterated that "any records obtained" by the Select Committee be transferred to the [Sub]Committee.[4] The Subcommittee is authorized to gather evidence on matters within its jurisdiction; specifically, with respect to congressional security and the accountability of legislative branch security.[5]

---

[1] Rule 10, Rules of the H.R., 118th Cong. (Jan. 10, 2023).
[2] 2 U.S.C. § 1965 (1996) (authority is granted to "the Committee on House Oversight" which, in 1999, was renamed the Committee on House Administration).
[3] H.R. Res. 503, 117th Cong. (2021); Letter from Nancy Pelosi, Speaker, H.R., to Bennie Thompson, Chairman of the Select Comm. to Investigate the Jan. 6th Attack on the U.S. Capitol (Dec. 29, 2022) (on file with the Subcommittee); H.R. Res. 5, 118th Cong. (2023); Rule 17, Rules of the Comm. on H. Admin. for the 118th Cong. (2023).
[4] Rule 19, Rules of the Comm. on H. Admin. for the 118th Cong. (2023).
[5] *Id.*

On June 30, 2021, the Democrat House majority passed House Resolution 503 establishing the Select Committee to Investigate the January 6th Attack on the United States Capitol.[6] The Select Committee, with its more than eighteen million dollar budget, resulted in little more than Hollywood-produced political theater and wasted taxpayer dollars to create an error-filled narrative masquerading as a congressional report.[7] Throughout its nearly two years of work, the Select Committee presented uncorroborated, cherry-picked evidence to build its narrative. The sole purpose of the Select Committee was to prevent President Trump from seeking reelection to the White House.

In contrast, Chairman Barry Loudermilk and the Committee on House Administration Subcommittee on Oversight ("Subcommittee") investigated the full array of security and intelligence breakdowns at the United States Capitol in the days leading up to, and on January 6, 2021. In the course of its investigation, the Subcommittee identified numerous inexcusable failures that should have been avoided, and must be addressed moving forward.

The events of January 6, 2021, were preventable. The politicization of Capitol security directly contributed to the many structural and procedural failures witnessed that day. Through the Subcommittee's robust oversight of the United States Capitol Police ("USCP") and supporting entities, the Subcommittee remains committed to ensuring necessary reforms to USCP operations and the Capitol's physical security.

Flawed Composition of the Select Committee

The day after the House voted on House Resolution 503 to create the Select Committee, Speaker Pelosi named seven Democrats and one Republican—Liz Cheney—to represent the interests of the Democrats.[8] Minority Leader Kevin McCarthy proposed five Republicans to represent the minority,[9] and in an outlandish and unprecedented move, Speaker Pelosi rejected the House minority leader's nominations.[10] Despite claiming to model the Select Committee after the Republican-led Select Committee on the Events Surrounding the 2012 Terrorist Attacks in Benghazi—wherein then-Minority Leader Pelosi appointed five Democrat members of her choosing to sit on that committee[11]—Speaker Pelosi refused to extend the same courtesy to

---

[6] H.R. Res. 503, 117th Cong. (2021).

[7] Warren Rojas, *House weaponization panel seeks to eclipse January 6 committee's $18M+ budget despite rocky start*, BUSINESS INSIDER (Mar. 8, 2023).

[8] STAFF OF H. SELECT COMM. TO INVESTIGATE THE JAN. 6TH ATTACK ON THE U.S. CAPITOL, 117TH CONG., FINAL REP. 30 (Comm. Print 2022).

[9] Marianna Sotomayor, et al., *Jim Jordan, four other Republicans chosen by House Minority Leader Kevin McCarthy to serve on panel investigating Jan. 6 riot*, WASH. POST (July 19, 2021).

[10] Press Release, NANCY PELOSI, Speaker, H.R., Pelosi Statement on Republican Recommendations to Serve on the Select Committee to Investigate the January 6th Attack on the U.S. Capitol (July 21, 2021).

[11] Jonathan Weisman & Jennifer Steinhauer, *Pelosi Picks 5 Democrats for Panel on Benghazi*, N.Y. TIMES (May 21, 2014).

Minority Leader McCarthy. She justified this radical move with this blanket excuse: "The unprecedented nature of January 6th demands this unprecedented decision."[12] Unfortunately for the American public, this excuse would be used by the Select Committee throughout the course of its existence to justify a multitude of untoward and unprecedented actions.

Minority Leader McCarthy refused to play along with Speaker Pelosi's clearly partisan Select Committee and withdrew all five of the Republican appointments.[13] As a result, Speaker Pelosi named Representative Adam Kinzinger—the only Republican other than Representative Cheney to vote in favor of the creation of the Select Committee—[14]as the ninth and final member of the Select Committee. According to House Rule 10 Clause 5, the members of standing committees shall be elected "from nomination[s] submitted by the respective party caucus or conference,"[15] but Speaker Pelosi ignored this rule. Despite H. Res 503 dictating that the Select Committee consist of thirteen members, five of whom in consultation with the minority leader, Speaker Pelosi pushed ahead with the seven Democrats and two Republicans, selected by the majority, who had demonstrated their commitment to the destruction of President Trump. For example, Representatives Jamie Raskin and Adam Schiff both served as impeachment managers against President Trump prior to their appointment to the Select Committee.[16]

The Select Committee's unwritten purpose was to prevent President Trump from seeking re-election in 2024. It was no secret that, after Speaker Pelosi failed to secure a conviction in the Senate for the second time, the only way to guarantee that President Trump could not return to office would be if he was found to have "engaged in an insurrection or rebellion against" the Constitution of the United States in violation of the Fourteenth Amendment.[17] This idea was published in major newspapers within days of January 6 and spoken about frequently in Left-wing circles.[18] Speaker Pelosi knew that the best pathway to stop President Trump from returning to the White House was if the Select Committee could craft a narrative compelling enough to convince the Department of Justice and the judicial system, along with the American public, that President Trump was an "insurrectionist."

House Resolution 503 mandated that the Select Committee investigate the "facts, circumstances, and causes" of January 6, and the "preparedness and response" of law enforcement.[19] Instead, as evidenced by the Select Committee's Final Report, it deployed its vast resources to attempt to

---

[12] Press Release, NANCY PELOSI, Speaker, H.R., Pelosi Statement on Republican Recommendations to Serve on the Select Committee to Investigate the January 6th Attack on the U.S. Capitol (July 21, 2021).

[13] *Minority Leader McCarthy News Conference on January 6 Committee*, C-SPAN (July 21, 2021).

[14] Luke Broadwater, *Pelosi Appoints Kinzinger to Panel Scrutinizing Jan. 6*, N.Y. TIMES (July 25, 2021).

[15] Rule 10(5)(a)(1), Rules of the H.R., 117th Cong. (2022).

[16] Press Release, JAMIE RASKIN, Representative, Speaker Pelosi Names Raskin Lead Impeachment Manager (Jan. 12, 2021); Press Release, ADAM SCHIFF, Representative, Schiff Statement on Being Named Lead House Impeachment Manager (Jan. 15, 2020).

[17] U.S. CONST. amend. XIV, § 3.

[18] Bruce Ackerman, *Impeachment won't keep Trump from running again. Here's a better way*, WASH. POST (Jan. 11, 2021).

[19] H.R. Res. 503, 117th Cong. § 3(1) (2021).

prevent President Trump from returning to the White House. H. Res. 503's mandate does not mention an investigation of President Trump, but the Select Committee still managed to include President Trump's name more than 1,900 times in its final report.

Replacing the Missing Ranking Member with a Pseudo "Vice Chair"

House Resolution 503 required the chairman of the Select Committee to consult with the "ranking minority member" for several important functions, including issuing subpoenas and ordering depositions.[20] The Select Committee did not have a ranking minority member.

The term "ranking minority member" has a clearly understood meaning under House Rules, and both parties have procedures for appointing ranking members to committees.[21] Both the Republican Conference and the Democratic Caucus Rules require their respective Steering Committees to first nominate members for the role of ranking member, and then the conference or caucus votes on those recommendations.[22] Without the Republicans sending any members to the Select Committee, there was no possibility for the Select Committee to regard either of the two Republicans on that committee as a "ranking member."

Instead, several months after the Select Committee was constituted and more than a month after its first hearing, Chair Bennie Thompson named Representative Liz Cheney as Vice Chair.[23] The position of vice chair is fundamentally distinct and functionally different than that of a ranking member.[24] Importantly, House Rules dictate that the vice chair of any standing or subcommittee be "[a] member of the majority party," and if the chair and vice chair are both unavailable, "the ranking majority member who is present shall preside."[25] In an effort to side-step the fatal absence of a ranking member, the Select Committee treated "Vice Chair" Cheney as the functional equivalent.

This obfuscation of the Select Committee's establishing rules alone may discredit its work. This issue has been raised in lawsuits challenging the authority of the Select Committee, but the courts chose to avoid the issue by asserting—sua sponte—the Speech or Debate Clause of the United States Constitution.[26] This follows the longstanding trend of Federal Courts deferring on issues within the two other branches of the federal government.[27] Because the courts will not interject to declare invalid the Select Committee's attempt to name a member of the opposing

---

[20] H.R. Res. 503, 117th Cong. § 5(c)(6)(A) (2021).

[21] Rule 14, Rules of the H. Repub. Conf., 117th Cong. (2021); Rule 21, Rules of the Dem. Caucus, 117th Cong. (2021).

[22] *Id.*

[23] Annie Grayer, et al., *Liz Cheney named vice chair of the January 6 select committee*, CNN (Sept. 2, 2021).

[24] Rule 14, Rules of the H. Repub. Conf., 117th Cong. (2021); Rule 21, Rules of the Dem. Caucus, 117th Cong. (2021).

[25] Rule 11, Rules of the H.R., 117th Cong. § (2)(d) (2021).

[26] Def. Mot. for Summ. J., at 18, Meadows v. Pelosi, 1:21-cv-3217-CJN (D.D.C.) (Oct. 31, 2022).

[27] *See, e.g.*, Baker v. Carr, 369 U.S. 186, 214 (1962) (courts are sensitive to the "respect due to a co-ordinate branch of the government.")

party as vice chair and have her assume—without authority and against House Rules—the role of ranking member, Congress itself must right its former wrongs and declare this appointment of Representative Cheney invalid now.

Select Committee's Unprecedented Exemption from Certain House Rules

House Democrats included an exemption to H. Rule 11 in the authorizing resolution that created the Select Committee.[28] Rule 11 required that committee rules provide equal time to the majority and minority party members to ask alternating questions.[29] Under Rule 11, committees "may adopt a rule" that gives members more than five minutes for questioning witnesses, but the extension would have had to apply equally to the majority and minority.[30] By removing Rule 11, House Democrats gave Chair Thompson unregulated power to run the Select Committee in ways that other committees could not, and effectively nullified any possibility of fairness even if Minority Leader McCarthy had been able to seat his original five Members.

Even with the exclusion of Rule 11, H. Res. 503 still required Chair Thompson to consult with the ranking member before issuing subpoenas or ordering depositions.[31] The Select Committee's exemption from some rules, and refusal to follow others, contribute to the dubious nature of its work and conclusions.

---

[28] H.R. Res. 503, 117th Cong. § 5(c)(1) (2021).
[29] Rule 11, Rules of the H.R., 117th Cong. (2021).
[30] *Id.*
[31] H.R. Res. 503, 117th Cong. § 5(c)(6)(A) (2021).

All committee chairs have the responsibility to archive noncurrent committee records at the end of each Congress.[32] It is a chair's responsibility to transfer these records to the Clerk of the House ("House Clerk"), who subsequently stores those records with the National Archives and Records Administration ("NARA").[33] The House Clerk's office generally holds these records for two years prior to sending them to NARA.[34] The resolution establishing the Select Committee added an additional reporting requirement by mandating all records of the committee be transferred to any committee designated by the Speaker of the House.[35] Days before the new Republican majority was sworn in, Speaker Pelosi sent a letter to Chair Thompson designating Select Committee records be transferred to the Committee on House Administration[36]. At the beginning of the 118th Congress, H. Res. 5 reiterated that all records from the Select Committee be transferred to the Committee on House Administration.[37]

Republicans on Chairman Loudermilk's Subcommittee immediately inventoried all records turned over by the Select Committee. This included both printed documents and digital records. During this initial document review, the Subcommittee determined that the Select Committee archived and provided roughly 270 transcribed interviews of witness testimonies and fewer than three terabytes of digital data.

House Rule 7 requires committees to submit noncurrent records to the House Clerk at the end of each Congress.[38] Under House Rule 7, it is the responsibility of "the chair of each committee" to "transfer to the House Clerk any noncurrent records of such committee."[39] House Rules continue to define noncurrent records as "an official, permanent record of the committee (including any record of a legislative, oversight, or other activity of such committee)."[40] The House Clerk specifies that depositions, transcripts, executive branch communications, and other similar recordings are among the records that should be archived pursuant to House Rules.[41]

Nevertheless, as part of its investigation, the Subcommittee learned that the Select Committee failed to archive or provide the Subcommittee with any of its video recordings of witness interviews, as many as 900 interview summaries or transcripts, more than one terabyte of digital data. Concerningly, of the documents that were archived, the Select Committee delivered more

---

[32] Rule 7, Rules of the H.R., 117th Cong. (2021).

[33] CONGRESSIONAL RESEARCH SERVICE, CRS Report R47590, ARCHIVAL RECORDS OF CONGRESS: FREQUENTLY ASKED QUESTIONS (Dec. 7, 2023).

[34] *Id.*

[35] H.R. Res. 503, 117th Cong. (2021).

[36] Letter from Nancy Pelosi, Speaker, H.R., to Bennie Thompson, Chairman, Select Comm. to Investigate the Jan. 6th Attack on the U.S. Capitol (Dec. 29, 2022) (on file with the Subcommittee).

[37] H.R. Res. 5, 118th Cong. (2023).

[38] Rule 7, Rules of the H.R., 118th Cong. (2023).

[39] *Id.*

[40] *Id.*

[41] H.R. OFF. OF THE CLERK, RECORDS MANAGEMENT MANUAL FOR COMMITTEES (Sept. 2023).

than 100 encrypted, password protected documents and never provided the passwords. It is unclear why the Select Committee chose only those documents to be shielded by password.

The failure to provide the Subcommittee with these records raises serious concerns about the content of the records and their contribution to the Select Committee's narrative. Furthermore, the failure to archive these records rests on Chair Thompson who had an obligation under House Rule 7 to "transfer to the Clerk any noncurrent records."[42] Failure to archive all noncurrent records, the corresponding transcripts, and the recovered password-protected encrypted files, is in violation of House Rules and obstructs the Subcommittee's investigation into Capitol security.

More Than One Terabyte of Missing Digital Data

Based on an inventory of this digital data and statements from Chair Thompson, the Subcommittee discovered that the Select Committee failed to archive more than one terabyte of digital data. In a July 7, 2022, letter to Chairman Loudermilk, Representative Thompson claimed that the Select Committee archived "over 4-terabyte[s]" of digital data.[43] However, after reviewing this archive file, the Subcommittee received less than three terabytes of digital data from the Select Committee. One terabyte is a substantial amount of missing data. One terabyte of data is equivalent to 6.5 million document pages such as PDFs or office files, 500 hours of high-definition video, or 250,000 photos.

Included in the physical files the Select Committee archived was a memorandum from the Select Committee's e-discovery platform contractor, dated December 28, 2022, in which the contractor explicitly states that the Select Committee excluded "Committee work-product" and "[select] documents the [Select Committee] deemed as sensitive" from its archiving process.[44] It is unclear what files were excluded, but it is clear that the Select Committee instructed its e-discovery contractor to proactively remove certain files from the archive it prepared and subsequently turned over to the Subcommittee.

Missing Video Recordings of Witness Interviews

Despite playing a prominent role in its hearings, the Select Committee refused to archive any of the video recordings it collected of witness interviews or depositions as required per House Rules.[45] During its primetime hearings, the Select Committee used numerous, selectively edited clips from these video recordings to build its pre-determined narrative. Representative Cheney

---

[42] Rule 7, Rules of the H.R., 118th Cong. (2023).

[43] Letter from Bennie Thompson, Representative, to Barry Loudermilk, Chairman, the Comm. on H. Admin. Oversight Subcomm. (July 7, 2022) (On file with the Subcommittee).

[44] Memorandum from Innovative Driven, Inc. to Nat'l Archives and Rec. Admin. (Dec. 28, 2022) (on file with the Subcommittee).

[45] H.R. Res. 503, 117th Cong. (2021); Letter from Nancy Pelosi, Speaker, H.R., to Bennie Thompson, Chairman, Select Comm. to Investigate the Jan. 6th Attack on the U.S. Capitol (Dec. 29, 2022) (on file with the Subcommittee); H.R. Res. 5, 118th Cong. (2023); Rule 17, Rules of the Comm. on H. Admin. for the 118th Cong. (2023); Rule 19, Rules of the Comm. on H. Admin. for the 118th Cong. (2023).

noted in her memoir that the Select Committee decided that reading witness transcripts during their primetime hearings was "unlikely to be effective," and instead they "needed the public to see" the witness on camera recounting their testimony.[46] According to Representative Cheney, the video recordings of their many interviews were indispensable to the Select Committee's efforts to convey its narrative.[47]

On June 26, 2023, Chairman Loudermilk sent Representative Thompson a letter seeking additional information about these recordings.[48] Representative Thompson replied on July 7, 2023, stating that the Select Committee did not archive any of the unedited video recordings of witness interviews or depositions.[49] Representative Thompson argued that the Select Committee was "not obligated to archive all video recordings of transcribed interviews or depositions."[50] Representative Thompson claimed this determination was based on guidance the Select Committee received from the House Clerk. However, according to official guidance from the House Clerk on what records should be archived, the list includes "video[s] of events, testimonies, and interviews."[51] Representative Thompson failed to produce any records of the guidance he claimed to have received.

Without the full videos of these transcribed interviews and depositions, neither the Subcommittee nor the American public are able to review and understand the full context of the video clips shown during the Select Committee's hearings. Similar to Representative Cheney's observation, printed transcripts do not convey emotion, movements, or voice inflections. The missing videos, along with the multitude of other missing documents and data that the Select Committee chose to withhold from further scrutiny, contribute to the Subcommittee's doubts of the accuracy and objectivity of the Select Committee's work.

Letters

- 5/26/23 Letter from Barry Loudermilk to Bennie Thompson
    - Select Committee Record Collection Inquiry
- 1/18/24 Letter from Barry Loudermilk to Bennie Thompson
    - Accessing Recovered Files Inquiry
- 5/18/23 Letter from Barry Loudermilk to Colleen Shogan
    - Select Committee Record Production Request
- 12/5/23 Letter from Barry Loudermilk to Bennie Thompson
    - Fulton County Inquiry

---

[46] LIZ CHENEY, OATH AND HONOR 244 (2023).

[47] *Id.*

[48] Letter from Barry Loudermilk, Chairman, Comm. on H. Admin. Oversight Subcomm., to Bennie Thompson, Representative (June 26, 2023) (on file with the Subcommittee).

[49] Letter from Bennie Thompson, Representative, to Barry Loudermilk, Chairman, Comm. on H. Admin. Oversight Subcomm. (July 7, 2023) (on file with the Subcommittee).

[50] *Id.*

[51] H.R. Off. of the Clerk, Rec. Mgmt. Manual for Comm's. (Sept. 2023).

- 1/8/24 Letter from Barry Loudermilk to Troy Nehls
  - Report Assistance Request
- 7/9/24 Letter from Barry Loudermilk to Colleen Shogan
  - In Camera Review Request
- 6/18/24 Letter from Barry Loudermilk to Muriel Bowser
  - Select Committee Record Production Request
- 6/18/24 Letter from Barry Loudermilk to Alejandro Mayorkas
  - Select Committee Record Production Request
- 6/18/24 Letter from Barry Loudermilk to Lloyd Austin
  - Select Committee Record Production Request
- 6/18/24 Letter from Barry Loudermilk to Deb Haaland
  - Select Committee Record Production Request
- 6/18/24 Letter from Barry Loudermilk to Merrick Garland
  - Select Committee Record Production Request
- 6/18/24 Letter from Barry Loudermilk to Antony Blinken
  - Select Committee Record Production Request
- 6/18/24 Letter from Barry Loudermilk to Jessica Rosenworcel
  - Select Committee Record Production Request
- 6/18/24 Letter from Barry Loudermilk to Sean Cooksey
  - Select Committee Record Production Request
- 6/18/24 Letter from Barry Loudermilk to Robin Carnahan
  - Select Committee Record Production Request
- 6/18/24 Letter from Barry Loudermilk to Colleen Shogan
  - Select Committee Record Production Request
- 6/18/24 Letter from Barry Loudermilk to Marcel Acosta
  - Select Committee Record Production Request
- 6/18/24 Letter from Barry Loudermilk to Daniel Hokanson
  - Select Committee Record Production Request
- 6/18/24 Letter from Barry Loudermilk to Rob Shriver
  - Select Committee Record Production Request
- 6/18/24 Letter from Barry Loudermilk to Pete Buttigieg
  - Select Committee Record Production Request
- 6/18/24 Letter from Barry Loudermilk to Janet Yellen
  - Select Committee Record Production Request
- 7/10/24 Letter from Barry Loudermilk to Kimberly Cheatle
  - Select Committee Record Production Request
- 11/8/24 Letter from Barry Loudermilk and Jim Jordan to Jack Smith
  - Trump Record Preservation Request

Representative Liz Cheney

Former Representative Elizabeth Cheney emerged as the principal figure driving the Select Committee's narrative. On May 12, 2021, Representative Cheney proudly stated, "I will do everything I can to ensure that the former president [Trump] never again gets anywhere near the Oval Office."[52] Six weeks later, Speaker Pelosi named Representative Cheney as one of her eight selections, and a founding member of the partisan Select Committee. Speaker Pelosi entrusted Representative Cheney to focus the Select Committee's efforts on diminishing President Trump's political future, and Representative Cheney delivered.

Representative Cheney mentions President Trump eighteen separate times in her four-page *Forward* to the Select Committee's Final Report—including her statements that "no man" who behaved as President Trump "can ever serve in any position of authority in our nation again," and that "[Trump] is unfit for any office."[53] In contrast, she fails to mention any of the tangible failures of that day. Representative Cheney spoke of law enforcement only twice, and never mentioned the National Guard or the multi-agency intelligence failures.[54] It appears as though Representative Cheney leveraged her unique position on the Select Committee to fulfill her promise "to do everything [she] can" to keep President Trump away from the Oval Office.

Representative Cheney's influence on the Select Committee's work and the conclusions it drew cannot be overstated. Before the Select Committee published its final report, fifteen current and former staffers approached the Washington Post to express deep frustration with Representative Cheney's heavy-handed oversight of the Select Committee's work.[55] The article states that "committee staff members were floored" when told that the final report "would focus almost entirely on Trump."[56] Another staff member stated, "when [the Select Committee] became a Cheney 2024 campaign, many of us became discouraged."[57] The article continues, "[p]eople familiar with the committee's work said Cheney has taken a far more hands-on role than [Chair] Bennie G. Thompson," and, "[s]he is said by multiple staffers to want the report to focus on Trump, and has pushed for the hearings to focus extensively on his conduct—and not what she views as other sideshows."[58] The Subcommittee's investigation revealed that few beyond Representative Cheney would consider the failures of senior Pentagon officials, general

---

[52] GUARDIAN NEWS, *Liz Cheney committed to ensure "Trump never gets near the Oval Office again,"* YOUTUBE (May 12, 2021).

[53] STAFF OF H. SELECT COMM. TO INVESTIGATE THE JAN. 6TH ATTACK ON THE U.S. CAPITOL, 117TH CONG., FINAL REP. 14-17 (Comm. Print 2022).

[54] *Id.* at 16-17.

[55] Jacqueline Alemany, et al., *Jan. 6 panel staffers angry at Cheney for focusing so much of report on Trump,* WASH. POST (Nov. 23, 2022).

[56] *Id.*

[57] *Id.*

[58] *Id.*

unpreparedness of Capitol Police, and the multiagency intelligence failures that contributed to the events of January 6 as "sideshows."

Representative Cheney's exhaustive efforts aside, the Select Committee initially struggled to produce a cohesive narrative that could lay the entirety of the blame on President Trump. The Select Committee needed a star witness who could be seen to give credibility to the narrative it was determined to convey. Through thousands of hours of interviews, and the interrogation of hundreds of witnesses, it is noteworthy that the Select Committee chose to focus the conclusions of its nearly one-thousand-page report largely on the uncorroborated and inconsistent testimony of one witness—Cassidy Hutchinson ("Hutchinson.") Hutchinson gave Representative Cheney and the other Members of the Select Committee exactly what they were looking for.

Cassidy Hutchinson

Cassidy Hutchinson was a twenty-four-year-old Special Assistant to the President and Coordinator for Legislative Affairs for White House Chief of Staff Mark Meadows ("Meadows") during his tenure as Chief of Staff—the position she held on January 6, 2021.[59] Prior to this position, she participated in the White House Internship Program[60] and then worked full-time as a staff assistant at the White House Office of Legislative Affairs.[61] According to testimony given to the Subcommittee by White House employees who worked closely with Hutchinson during her time in Meadows' office, her responsibilities consisted primarily of accompanying Meadows throughout the day, organizing his schedule, and other administrative duties within the office. She communicated regularly with other White House employees to plan and organize Meadows' calendar, and she had a desk located near the doorway leading to Meadows' office.

Despite initial reporting that Hutchinson became unemployed for a period of time at the end of the first Trump Administration,[62] it was revealed that Hutchinson continued to work as a "coordinator for [President] Trump's official, taxpayer-funded, post presidential office" from about "January 20, 2021, to April 1, 2021," and earned an annualized salary of $90,000 for that work, according to the Government Services Administration.[63] Among the many unsubstantiated claims made by Hutchinson throughout her interactions with Representative Cheney and the Select Committee, Hutchinson proclaimed that she was "disgusted" by President Trump's actions and called his activity "unpatriotic" and "un-American."[64] It is noteworthy, then, that Hutchinson

---

[59] EXEC. OFF. OF THE PRESIDENT, ANN. REP. TO CONG. ON WHITE HOUSE OFF. PERS. (June 26, 2020).

[60] Brian McGuire, *A Captain in the 'People's House,'* CHRISTOPHER NEWPORT UNIV. (Oct. 18, 2018).

[61] Sam Woodward, *Who is Cassidy Hutchinson, the Meadows aide who testified before Congress?*, CNN (updated June 28, 2022, 3:25 PM).

[62] John Wagner, et al., *Who is Cassidy Hutchinson?* WASH. POST (updated June 30, 2022, 12:35 PM).

[63] Dave Levinthal & C. Ryan Barber, *EXCLUSIVE: Cassidy Hutchinson kept working for Donald Trump for 9 weeks after he left the White House, government records show,* BUS. INSIDER (Aug. 1, 2022).

[64] *On the Jan. 6th Investigation: Hearing before the H. Select Comm. to Investigate the Jan. 6th Attack on the U.S. Capitol,* 117th Cong. (2022) (testimony of Cassidy Hutchinson).

continued working for President Trump for nine weeks after his presidency, despite the testimony she gave against his character and actions surrounding January 6.

Multiple reports alleged that Hutchinson planned to move to Mar-a-Lago with President Trump and form part of his post-presidential staff.[65] However, President Trump came to believe that Hutchinson was responsible for leaking the list of employees he planned to have work for him in Florida, and he personally disinvited Hutchinson from moving.[66] Before the Select Committee was formed, President Trump had heard negative things about Hutchinson, including that she was "a total phony and 'leaker.'"[67] In a post on his Truth Social, he asked "[w]hy did she want to go with us [to Florida] if she felt we were so terrible?"[68] The Subcommittee was unable to identify an answer to this question.

Cassidy Hutchinson claimed that Meadows informed her in the final days of the administration that she was not going to continue working for President Trump at Mar-a-Lago.[69] It is unclear when she had her last day as an employee for President Trump, but it remains a fact that nearly a year after the events of January 6, 2021, she contacted the Trump team to obtain an attorney to help represent her before the inquests of the Select Committee.[70]

Representative Cheney's Initial Interactions with Cassidy Hutchinson

The Select Committee began its investigation by interviewing hundreds of individuals it believed were connected to the events of January 6, 2021. Hutchinson was one of those individuals. Hutchinson could not afford an attorney, so she contacted two close allies of President Trump, Eric Herschmann and Alex Cannon, who secured attorney Stefan Passantino ("Passantino") to represent Hutchinson at no cost to her.[71] Initially, Hutchinson gave two under-oath testimonies, each lasting several hours.[72] Those two lengthy-yet-largely-insignificant interviews with Hutchinson brought her limited notoriety, with several news outlets attributing claims of

[65] Jennifer Jacobs & Saleha Moshin, *Trump Plans to Live at Mar-a-Lago, Employ Some Current Aides*, BLOOMBERG (updated Jan. 15, 2021, 8:02 PM); Philip Rucker, et al., *Trump to flee Washington and seek rehabilitation in a MAGA oasis: Florida*, WASH. POST (Jan. 16, 2021, 5:01 PM).

[66] Donald Trump (@realDonaldTrump), TRUTH SOCIAL (June 28, 2022, 6:02 PM).

[67] *Id.*

[68] *Id.*

[69] CASSIDY HUTCHINSON, ENOUGH 229 (2023).

[70] Select Comm. to Investigate the Jan. 6th Attack on the U.S. Capitol, Transcribed Interview of Cassidy Hutchinson (Sept. 14, 2022).

[71] Select Comm. to Investigate the Jan. 6th Attack on the U.S. Capitol, Transcribed Interview of Cassidy Hutchinson (Feb. 23, 2022); Select Comm. to Investigate the Jan. 6th Attack on the U.S. Capitol, Transcribed Interview of Cassidy Hutchinson (Sept. 14, 2022).

[72] Select Comm. to Investigate the Jan. 6th Attack on the U.S. Capitol, Transcribed Interview of Cassidy Hutchinson (Feb. 23, 2022); Select Comm. to Investigate the Jan. 6th Attack on the U.S. Capitol, Transcribed Interview of Cassidy Hutchinson (Mar. 7, 2022).

Republican politicians seeking pardons and foreknowledge of violence leading up to January 6 to Hutchinson.[73]

Following her second interview, Hutchinson drastically switched her narrative and began testifying to a variety of unsubstantiated and uncorroborated claims that ultimately appeared in the Select Committee's final report. It is not entirely clear why Hutchinson suddenly altered her testimony, but the Subcommittee has uncovered evidence of secret conversations between Hutchinson, former White House employee Alyssa Farah Griffin ("Farah Griffin"), and, troublingly, conversations between Hutchinson and Representative Cheney without the knowledge of Hutchinson's attorney.[74]

Alyssa Farah Griffin Backchanneled with Vice Chair Liz Cheney to Help Hutchinson Change her Story

For nearly a month, Farah Griffin acted as an intermediary between Vice Chair Cheney and the Select Committee's star witness, Hutchinson. As an intermediary, Farah Griffin helped coordinate Hutchinson's third transcribed interview—without the knowledge of Hutchinson's attorney, Stefan Passantino.[75] In a television panel with a member of the Select Committee—Representative Raskin—a year following the end of the Select Committee, Hutchinson freely stated that she had "backchanneled for a third interview without my former attorney's knowledge at the time, with one of my good friends, Alyssa Farah Griffin."[76] At this time, Farah Griffin and Hutchinson discussed the optics of Hutchinson leaking "new information" to the press instead of testifying directly to the Select Committee.[77] Hutchinson's messages indicate that she and Farah Griffin colluded to create a false story about why Hutchinson needed to do a third transcribed interview for the Select Committee to convince her attorney, Passantino.[78]

---

[73] Kyle Cheney & Nicholas Wu, *GOP lawmakers were deeply involved in Trump plans to overturn election, new evidence suggests*, POLITICO (Apr. 23, 2022); Luke Broadwater & Alan Feuer, *Meadows Was Warned Jan. 6 Could Turn Violent, House Panel Says*, N. Y. TIMES (Apr. 23, 2022).

[74] Press Release, COMM. ON H. ADMIN. OVERSIGHT SUBCOMM., New Texts Reveal Liz Cheney Communicated with Cassidy Hutchinson About Her Select Committee Testimony—Without Hutchinson's Attorney's Knowledge—Despite Cheney Knowing it was Unethical (Oct. 15, 2024).

[75] *Id.*

[76] *Enough: Former Special Assistant to President Trump Cassidy Hutchinson spoke about being in the White House on January 5, 2021, and her subsequent testimony to the Select Committee. George Washington University and Politics and Prose Bookstore in Washington, D.C., hosted this event.* C-SPAN (Oct. 9, 2023).

[77] Press Release, COMM. ON H. ADMIN. OVERSIGHT SUBCOMM., New Texts Reveal Liz Cheney Communicated with Cassidy Hutchinson About Her Select Committee Testimony—Without Hutchinson's Attorney's Knowledge—Despite Cheney Knowing it was Unethical (Oct. 15, 2024).

[78] *Id.*

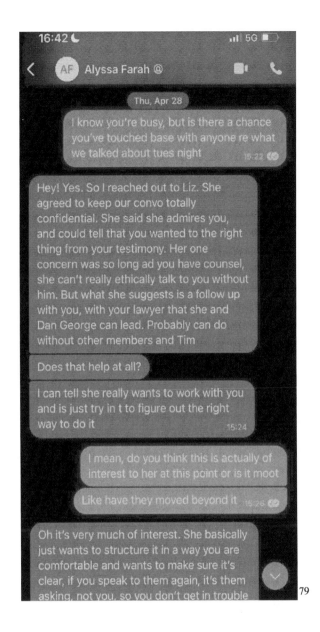

In her May 17, 2021, transcribed interview, Hutchinson testified to a series of uncorroborated and unverified stories that conveniently fit the Select Committee's anti-Trump narrative. Despite already testifying to the Select Committee twice, Hutchinson never previously mentioned this "new information."

[79] Cassidy Hutchinson, private Signal text conversation with Alyssa Farah Griffin. (Apr. 28, 2022) (on file with the Subcommittee).

The Subcommittee was only able to obtain a limited number of text messages from Hutchinson and Farah Griffin, but Representative Cheney's influence on Hutchinson is apparent from that point forward by her dramatic change in testimony and eventual claims against President Trump using second- and thirdhand accounts. For example, Hutchinson claimed that White House Deputy Chief of Staff Anthony Ornato ("Ornato") told her that Trump lunged towards the driver of his car after Trump's request to go to the Capitol was denied. This story has never been corroborated and was directly refuted by both United States Secret Service ("USSS") agents in the vehicle with President Trump that day, and Ornato himself.

Vice Chair Liz Cheney Continued Communicating Directly with Cassidy Hutchinson Despite Problematic Ethical Implications

After her third transcribed interview, Hutchinson reached out to Representative Cheney directly.[80] While Hutchinson revealed the general timing of these conversations in her book, the extent and content of their communication was not previously disclosed until they were uncovered by Chairman Loudermilk.[81] When Hutchinson texted Representative Cheney, she was still represented by Passantino, which Representative Cheney knew. Representative Cheney and Hutchinson communicated directly for days without Passantino's knowledge.

It is unusual—and potentially unethical—for a Member of Congress conducting an investigation to contact a witness if the Member knows that the individual is represented by legal counsel. Representative Cheney is an attorney, and an attorney who circumvents an individual's legal representation would violate well-established attorney ethics standards and the Washington D.C. Bar Rules of Professional Conduct, regardless of who initiates the contact. [82] While it is not clear how the D.C. Bar would apply this rule to an attorney who also sits as a Member of Congress, its rules state that "a lawyer shall not communicate or cause another to communicate about the subject of the representation with a person known to be represented by another lawyer in the matter. . . ."[83] This appears to be precisely what Representative Cheney did at this time, and within a matter of days of these secret conversations, Hutchinson would go on to recant her previous testimony and introduce her most outlandish claims.

It must be emphasized that Representative Cheney would likely have known her communications without the knowledge of Hutchinson's attorney were illicit and unethical at that time. Farah

---

[80] Cassidy Hutchinson, private Signal text conversation with Liz Cheney, Representative. (June 6, 2022) (on file with the Subcommittee).

[81] Press Release, COMM. ON H. ADMIN. OVERSIGHT SUBCOMM., New Texts Reveal Liz Cheney Communicated with Cassidy Hutchinson About Her Select Committee Testimony—Without Hutchinson's Attorney's Knowledge—Despite Cheney Knowing it was Unethical (Oct. 15, 2024).

[82] D.C. BAR R. PRO. CONDUCT, 4.2(a); *See, e.g.*, Wallace E. Shipp, Jr., WASHINGTON D.C. OFFICE OF BAR COUNSEL, in re Anne P. Hovis, Esquire (July 13, 2011) (the Washington D.C. barred attorney knew that a party was represented by counsel in the matter but communicated with the party directly. The attorney even denigrated the party's attorney and suggested she obtain new counsel. This case bears a striking resemblance to Representative Cheney's communications with the represented party Hutchinson).

[83] D.C. BAR R. PRO. CONDUCT, 4.2(a).

Griffin indicated as much in her previously-mentioned message to Hutchinson on April 28, 2022, when she wrote that Representative Cheney's "one concern" was that as long as Hutchinson was represented by counsel, "she [Cheney] can't really ethically talk to you [Hutchinson] without him [Passantino]."[84] Despite Representative Cheney's initial hesitation, the Subcommittee uncovered evidence of frequent, direct conversations between Hutchinson and Representative Cheney without Passantino's knowledge, and also through their intermediary Farah Griffin.[85]

Understandably, Representative Cheney attempted to distance herself from the appearance of impropriety in her memoir published in the aftermath of the Select Committee. In her words, she was "sympathetic to [Hutchinson's] situation, but [Representative Cheney] did not want our committee to be advising her on what to do next."[86] It remains to be determined why Representative Cheney would allegedly avoid communicating with Hutchinson in April because of her commitment to ethics but would communicate with her frequently under those same circumstances in May and June as the date of their televised hearing grew closer.

Vice Chair Cheney Covertly Assisted Hutchinson and Influenced Her to Fire Her Attorney

Representative Cheney's influence on Hutchinson went beyond contacting Hutchinson directly. Representative Cheney played a primary role in Hutchinson firing her current, free-to-her legal counsel Passantino, and even provided Hutchinson with a list of attorneys that would likely contribute to building the Select Committee's narrative.[87] The account of how Hutchinson terminated her counsel and hired new counsel varies in important ways between Hutchinson's and Representative Cheney's respective memoirs, both published in the aftermath of the Select Committee.

According to Representative Cheney, her concerns for respecting ethical boundaries limited her contribution to Hutchinson's strategy and she passively waited for Hutchinson to fire her attorney and find new counsel on her own.

[84] Cassidy Hutchinson, private Signal text conversation with Alyssa Farah Griffin. (Apr. 28, 2022) (on file with the Subcommittee).

[85] Press Release, COMM. ON H. ADMIN. OVERSIGHT SUBCOMM., New Texts Reveal Liz Cheney Communicated with Cassidy Hutchinson About Her Select Committee Testimony—Without Hutchinson's Attorney's Knowledge—Despite Cheney Knowing it was Unethical (Oct. 15, 2024).

[86] Cassidy Hutchinson, private Signal text conversation with Alyssa Farah Griffin. (Apr. 28, 2022) (on file with the Subcommittee).

[87] CASSIDY HUTCHINSON, ENOUGH 295 (2023).

> Not long after this third interview, Cassidy contacted me directly. She told me that she was inclined to represent herself going forward. I was very sympathetic to her situation, but I did not want our committee to be advising her on what she should do next. I told Cassidy that she could consult another lawyer, and seek his or her independent advice on how best to move forward. Every witness deserves an attorney who will represent their interests exclusively. [88]

Unfortunately for Representative Cheney, Hutchinson published her own memoir and recounted a different set of circumstances. In her book *Enough*, Hutchinson stated that not only did Representative Cheney play an integral part in Hutchinson's developing testimony but even provided Hutchinson with a list of attorneys to replace her current counsel. [89]

> I asked if she or any of the members or committee staff might know an attorney who would be willing to put me on a payment plan. Liz said that she would follow up after she spoke with colleagues.
>
> The next day, she called and provided me with contact information for multiple attorneys at various firms. I thanked her and promised that I would figure out a way to do the right thing, regardless of the outcome of the search for new counsel. I could not find the words to tell her that the committee was giving me one of the greatest gifts I could have received: hope.

[90]

Far from passively observing, Representative Cheney took an active role in securing Select Committee-friendly attorneys to represent Hutchinson. "The next day, she [Representative Cheney] called and provided me [Hutchinson] with contact information for multiple attorneys at various firms."[91] In addition, the Signal messages recovered by Chairman Loudermilk demonstrate that Representative Cheney and Hutchinson spoke directly with one another several days before Hutchinson ultimately terminated her attorney.[92] What other information was communicated during these phone calls may never be known, but what is known is that Representative Cheney consciously attempted to minimize her contact with Hutchinson in her book, and the most likely reason to try to bury that information would be if Representative

---

[88] LIZ CHENEY, OATH AND HONOR 310 (2023).
[89] CASSIDY HUTCHINSON, ENOUGH 295 (2023).
[90] LIZ CHENEY, OATH AND HONOR 310 (2023).
[91] CASSIDY HUTCHINSON, ENOUGH 295 (2023).
[92] Press Release, COMM. ON H. ADMIN. OVERSIGHT SUBCOMM., New Texts Reveal Liz Cheney Communicated with Cassidy Hutchinson About Her Select Committee Testimony—Without Hutchinson's Attorney's Knowledge—Despite Cheney Knowing it was Unethical (Oct. 15, 2024).

Cheney knew that it was improper and unethical to communicate with Hutchinson without her counsel present.

On June 9, 2022, Hutchinson formally ended her attorney-client relationship with her first attorney, Stefan Passantino.[93] That same day, she retained attorneys Bill Jordan and Jody Hunt of Alston & Bird, at the recommendation of Representative Cheney.[94]

In a twist of irony, Representative Cheney spoke out forcefully against individuals who endeavored to influence witness testimony in the Select Committee. At the end of the Select Committee hearing in which Hutchinson testified, Representative Cheney stated, "[l]et me say one more time, we will take any effort to influence witness testimony very seriously."[95] In an interview with ABC News the following day, Representative Cheney reportedly stated that the Select Committee "may make a criminal referral to the Justice Department, recommending that anybody attempting to influence witness testimony before the [Select] Committee be prosecuted for witness tampering."[96] Whether lacking in self-awareness or to obfuscate her own furtive behavior, it is consistent with the Select Committee's practice of lodging accusations against President Trump and those associated with him as if those accusations are fact, when the Select Committee itself was engaged in the very behavior it had accused of President Trump.

Cassidy Hutchinson's Four Subsequent Interviews and Live Testimony

On June 20, 2022—less than two weeks after Hutchinson fired Passantino and hired the attorneys Representative Cheney suggested—Hutchinson sat for her fourth transcribed interview with the Select Committee under unusual circumstances. Prior to this interview, nearly every interview the Select Committee conducted included approximately a dozen people—including committee staff members, committee counsel, often a Member of the Select Committee, the interviewee, and the interviewee's legal representation. Most of the interviews were done in large conference rooms or over zoom, allowing space for all participants. Hutchinson's fourth transcribed interview, however, was vastly different. It consisted of only four people: Representative Cheney, one attorney from the Select Committee, Hutchinson, and Hutchinson's new counsel. Additionally, instead of the Select Committee conducting the interview in a conference room or virtually, Representative Cheney used her private hideaway inside of the United States Capitol Building.[97]

In light of the extravagant nature of the claims Hutchinson made during her third and fourth interviews, it would be prudent for the Select Committee to invest a portion of its substantial

[93] Select Comm. to Investigate the Jan. 6th Attack on the U.S. Capitol, Transcribed Interview of Cassidy Hutchinson, (Sept. 14, 2022).
[94] *Id.*
[95] Libby Cathey, *Trump tried to call Jan. 6 committee witness, Cheney says,* ABC NEWS (Aug. 4, 2022).
[96] Reuters Staff, *Jan. 6 committee may make criminal referral on witness tampering,* REUTERS (July 2, 2022).
[97] Select Comm. to Investigate the Jan. 6th Attack on the U.S. Capitol, Transcribed Interview of Cassidy Hutchinson, (June 20, 2022).

resources into investigating the veracity of Hutchinson's second and thirdhand accounts, but Representative Cheney decided instead to rush Hutchinson's narrative into the public domain. Just days before Hutchinson's public testimony, the Select Committee had revised its schedule to postpone hearings for several weeks. Instead, Representative Cheney scheduled an "emergency public hearing"[98] to create the appearance of urgency. Six days after Hutchinson's fourth interview, on June 26, 2022, Representative Cheney gave Hutchinson and her new attorney Bill Jordan a preparatory walkthrough of the Canon Caucus Room.[99] Hutchinson testified the following day, during network television primetime, on June 28.[100] According to public reporting, and to the consternation of Select Committee staff, Cheney's decision to rush Hutchinson's testimony caused "unforced errors" and did not afford staff the "opportunity to thoroughly vet the line of questioning."[101]

It is no surprise that the claims made in Hutchinson's first two sworn interviews vary substantially from the claims she made following Representative Cheney's direct intervention. Her first two interviews, though consistent with one another, were significantly different than the narrative she told in her four subsequent interviews and live testimony. This change may also explain why the Select Committee released the text of Hutchinson's transcribed interviews in reverse order, with the testimony most helpful to its messaging published first, and her first two interviews—which contradicted her later elaborate claims—published only five days before the end of the Select Committee.[102] The Select Committee needed a witness who could provide the vehicle for the message it desired to convey, and Hutchinson's sensational new testimony gave the Select Committee exactly what it was seeking.

At the beginning of its investigation, the Subcommittee reached out to the FBI requesting Hutchinson's FD-302—a report used by agents to summarize and record information from interviews—to compare the testimony she gave to the FBI to the testimony she gave to the Select Committee.[103] To date, the FBI has not responded to the Subcommittee's request.

Select Committee Findings and Evidence that Disprove Cassidy Hutchinson's Allegations

Despite the Select Committee's exhaustive interviews of hundreds of witnesses, Cassidy Hutchinson was the only witness to testify to a series of specific, outrageous claims about President Trump on January 6, 2021. Nearly all her allegations involve incidents to which she

---

[98] Katherine Faulders, *Jan. 6 committee unexpectedly adds hearing for Tuesday*, ABC NEWS (June 27, 2022, 4:33 PM).

[99] CASSIDY HUTCHINSON, ENOUGH 310 (2023).

[100] *On the Jan. 6th Investigation: Hearing before the H. Select Comm. to Investigate the Jan. 6th Attack on the U.S. Capitol,* 117th Cong. (2022).

[101] Jacqueline Alemany, et al., *Jan. 6 panel staffers angry at Cheney for focusing so much of report on Trump,* WASH. POST (Nov. 23, 2022).

[102] Press Release, SELECT COMM. TO INVESTIGATE THE JAN. 6 ATTACK ON THE U.S. CAPITOL, *Release of Select Committee Materials* (Dec. 22, 2022).

[103] Letter from Barry Loudermilk, Chairman, Comm. on H. Admin. Oversight Subcomm., to Christopher Wray, Director, Federal Bureau of Investigation (Apr. 11, 2024) (on file with the Subcommittee).

was not an eyewitness, and the parties she credited for relaying those alleged events to her categorically denied her claims. Ultimately, Chairman Loudermilk and the Subcommittee uncovered evidence—evidence available to the Select Committee—disproving her eight most sensational claims. Hutchinson's willingness to testify under oath to these demonstrably false claims proves her unreliability as a witness. The Select Committee's decision to craft its narrative almost exclusively on the unchallenged, uncorroborated claims of one witness fails to meet even the most basic investigative standards and as a result the Select Committee's Final Report lacks any credibility.

FINDING 1: President Trump did not attack his Secret Service detail at any time on January 6.

FINDING 2: There was no pre-planned off-the-record move to the Capitol in the days leading up to January 6.

FINDING 3: There is no evidence that President Trump agreed with rioters chanting "hang Mike Pence."

FINDING 4: Cassidy Hutchinson falsely claimed to have drafted a handwritten note for President Trump on January 6.

FINDING 5: President Trump did not have intelligence indicating violence on the morning of January 6.

FINDING 6: Cassidy Hutchinson lied about the classification status of documents to disparage Mark Meadows.

FINDING 7: Representative Cheney and Cassidy Hutchinson attempted to disbar Stefan Passantino.

FINDING 8: Cassidy Hutchinson misrepresented President Trump's actions at Lafayette Square Park in the summer of 2020.

FINDING 1: President Trump did not attack his Secret Service detail at any time on January 6.

Perhaps the most memorable of Cassidy Hutchinson's allegations about President Trump's behavior on January 6 was the contention that President Trump attempted to seize the steering wheel from the control of the driver of his Secret Service detail, and when that was unsuccessful, Hutchinson claimed that he lunged toward the neck of the other agent in the vehicle. This hoax dominated the news cycle for several weeks.[104] She said to have heard this story thirdhand—from Tony Ornato ("Ornato"), who heard it from Robert "Bobby" Engel ("Engel"), who was one of the agents who rode in President Trump's vehicle. In her public testimony before the Select Committee, Hutchinson stated:

> When the car started moving, I'm under the impression, from the story as Tony had retold it, it just made Mr. Trump irate, and he lunged forward into what I believe is the -- would be called the cab of the Presidential limo and went to grab at the steering wheel. And Bobby had said, "Sir, I'm going to need you to take your hand off. We're going back to the White House. That's final."
>
> Mr. Trump again was extremely angry at that response and used his free hand, to my understanding, to then lunge at Bobby Engel.

[105]

Hutchinson motioned towards her clavicle while describing the alleged incident,[106] as if to indicate that President Trump had "lunged" at his own detail's neck somewhere along the drive from the Ellipse to the White House—a drive that takes no more than one minute to complete. The Select Committee previously conducted transcribed interviews, under oath, with Engel and Ornato, and neither of those two witnesses made any mention of an attack or rage on that short drive.[107]

Both Ornato and Engel, as well as the Secret Service agent driving the vehicle, spoke out to categorically deny Hutchinson's story the same day as Hutchinson's public testimony to the Select Committee.[108] It is unclear to the Subcommittee why the Select Committee did not seek to corroborate Hutchinson's story by conducting follow-up interviews with Ornato or Engel, or

---

[104] Allan Smith & Peter Alexander, *Former Meadows aide: Trump lunged at Secret Service agent, tried to grab steering wheel on Jan. 6*, NBC NEWS (updated June 28, 2022, 11:04 PM).

[105] *On the Jan. 6th Investigation: Hearing before the H. Select Comm. to Investigate the Jan. 6th Attack on the U.S. Capitol*, 117th Cong. (2022).

[106] *Id.*

[107] *Id.*

[108] Allan Smith & Peter Alexander, *Former Meadows Aide: Trump lunged at Secret Service agent, tried to grab steering wheel on Jan. 6*, NBC NEWS (updated June 28, 2022, 11:04 PM).

interviewing the driver, before going public with Hutchinson's thirdhand testimony. Those three eyewitnesses to her allegations were not interviewed again by the Select Committee for more than four months after Hutchinson's hearing.[109] The Select Committee chose to promote Hutchinson's version of events—citing a series of other unnamed individuals who were further removed from the alleged incident than even Hutchinson—over that of two federal law enforcement agents who were the only possible eyewitnesses.

In his November interview—nearly five months after Hutchinson's testimony—Engel said this about the alleged attack:

Q	All right.
	Do you remember him -- any kind of physical gesture, any kind of lunge, any kind of gesture at all, when he was told he couldn't go to the Capitol?
A	No, sir.
Q	Was he agitated?
A	I didn't sense him as being agitated.
Q	Was there a heated argument in the Suburban?
A	No, sir.
Q	Was the President irate?
A	I would not describe him as irate.[110]

The Select Committee did not give President Trump's Secret Service driver the opportunity to give his recollection of those events until November 2022.[111] He testified that he had not been contacted by the Select Committee in any way until that time. The driver testified to the following:

---

[109] Select Comm. to Investigate the Jan. 6th Attack on the U.S. Capitol, Transcribed Interview of Robert Engel (Nov. 17, 2022); Select Comm. to Investigate the Jan. 6th Attack on the U.S. Capitol, Transcribed Interview of U.S. Secret Service Agent (Nov. 7, 2022); Select Comm. to Investigate the Jan. 6th Attack on the U.S. Capitol, Transcribed Interview of Anthony Ornato (Nov. 29, 2022).
[110] Select Comm. to Investigate the Jan. 6th Attack on the U.S. Capitol, Transcribed Interview of Robert Engel (Nov. 17, 2022).
[111] Select Comm. to Investigate the Jan. 6th Attack on the U.S. Capitol, Transcribed Interview of U.S. Secret Service Agent [p.164] (Nov. 7, 2022).

> A So prior to June 28th, which I believe was Cassidy Hutchinson testimony in
>
> front of the committee, I had not been interviewed by any investigative body or the
>
> Secret Service internally concerning any of the events that had happened on January 6th.
>
> And then obviously on June 28th, in a public hearing of this committee, Cassidy
>
> Hutchinson made accusations or relayed accusations that the President of the United
>
> States had tried to commandeer his limousine by grabbing the steering wheel and
>
> assaulted Mr. Engel.
>
> I was in the car. Obviously, I was driving. Neither of those things happened. [112]

Waiting nearly five months to interview the two Secret Service agents and Ornato, who could verify Hutchinson's story, is unjustifiable. In addition to the Select Committee's apparent lack of interest in verifying its most sensational claims, the Members of the Select Committee demonstrated a steady determination to its narrative despite the ever-increasing exculpatory evidence and the outright denials by each of the eyewitnesses. The driver clearly stated, "[n]either of those things happened."[113]

In response, Representative Cheney asked the driver a question alluding that the driver did not understand Hutchinson's testimony.

> Ms. Cheney. Thanks, Mr. Harris.
>
> First of all, I just want to thank the special agent very much for his testimony, for
>
> his -- for his service and for his testimony today.   I just wanted to ask, though, is it the
>
> special agent's understanding that Ms. Hutchinson's testimony to the committee was that
>
> there had been an actual physical assault in the SUV? [114]

Representative Cheney's efforts to distinguish between a physical assault and a physical altercation is significant. If Hutchinson's version of events conflicted with the firsthand accounts

---

[112] *Id.*

[113] Select Comm. to Investigate the Jan. 6th Attack on the U.S. Capitol, Transcribed Interview of U.S. Secret Service Agent (Nov. 7, 2022).

[114] *Id.*

of the other witnesses, it would damage Representative Cheney's desired narrative. In an effort to rehabilitate Hutchinson's testimony in the face of contradictory firsthand accounts, Representative Cheney attempted to draw a distinction between Hutchinson's words and the actual witness' recollection. A physical assault has a legal criminal definition and is more substantial. A physical altercation, on the other hand, is obscure and subjective. Representative Cheney described the alleged event as a physical altercation during Hutchinson's public testimony,[115] but conveniently called it an assault in the Secret Service driver's interview, knowing the agent would deny the stronger language.

> Ms. Cheney.   And, despite this altercation, this physical altercation during the
>
> ride back to the White House, President Trump still demanded to go to the Capitol.
> [116]

Unfortunately for the Select Committee's narrative—the narrative that President Trump was unhinged and willing to get into physical altercations with his Secret Service detail—the driver's declaration that "[n]either of those things happened"[117] left no room to doubt that Hutchinson's thirdhand accounting of the event was baseless.

FINDING 2: There was no pre-planned off-the-record move to the Capitol in the days leading up to January 6.

The Select Committee claimed there was a plan in place for President Trump to go to the Capitol after his speech at the Ellipse.[118] The Subcommittee has reviewed more than fifteen interview transcripts from White House and Secret Service employees that contradict the notion of a Secret Service plan to go to the Capitol. Outside of a brief mention of the idea, the move was merely a rumor blown out of proportion by the Select Committee.

> Ms. Cheney.   As we have all just heard, in the days leading up to January 6th, on
>
> the day of the speech, both before and during and after the rally speech, President Trump
>
> was pushing his staff to arrange for him to come up here to the Capitol during the
>
> electoral vote count.
> [119]

---

[115] *On the Jan. 6th Investigation: Hearing before the H. Select Comm. to Investigate the Jan. 6th Attack on the U.S. Capitol*, 117th Cong. (2022).

[116] *Id.*

[117] Select Comm. to Investigate the Jan. 6th Attack on the U.S. Capitol, Transcribed Interview of U.S. Secret Service Agent (Nov. 7, 2022).

[118] *On the Jan. 6th Investigation: Hearing before the H. Select Comm. to Investigate the Jan. 6th Attack on the U.S. Capitol*, 117th Cong. (2022).

[119] *Id.*

Many agents "at the highest levels within the Secret Service" testified to the Select Committee that an off the record ("OTR") move to the Capitol was never more than a rumor, casually raised on January 4, 2021, and never seriously considered.[120] The Select Committee hid these transcripts. Although the Select Committee's report alludes that the OTR move to the Capitol was a matter of fact, buried in a footnote in the same report, the Select Committee admits the following:

> Despite the fact that the prospect of an OTR to the Capitol was raised at the highest levels within the Secret Service, some of its highest-ranking agents insisted to the Select Committee that they did not recall any such discussions on the day of January 6th.

[121]

See the full account by Robert Engel, head of President Trump's Secret Service detail, explaining that the idea of an OTR was a *hypothetical* from Bobby Peede—the Director of Presidential Advance—that never seriously came up again:[122]

> A   I didn't take Bobby Peede's question to me as a notification that the President wanted to go to the Capitol.   I interpreted his question to me as a hypothetical, or a what-if type of situation.   And maybe that was Bobby Peede's intent to just test the waters with me to find out if the Service would be amicable to doing something like that, and then go back to wherever he was going to go back to to say, well, the Service says they can't do it.   I don't know.
>
> I just -- my -- that's how I interpreted Bobby Peede's request, not as an order, not as a "you have to do this," not as the President wants to do this.   I interpreted it as a hypothetical or a what-if request.   And, therefore, my response back to him was, No, it's something that we're not going to be able to do.

---

[120] STAFF OF H. SELECT COMM. TO INVESTIGATE THE JAN. 6TH ATTACK ON THE U.S. CAPITOL, 117TH CONG., FINAL REP. 587 n.76 (Comm. Print 2022).

[121] *Id.*

[122] Select Comm. to Investigate the Jan. 6th Attack on the U.S. Capitol, Transcribed Interview of Robert Engel (Mar. 4, 2022).

It is clear that once again, Hutchinson's testimony about the OTR and the physical altercation in the Beast is refuted by multiple sources and corroborated by none, yet the Select Committee still relied heavily on her testimony throughout their investigation and in their final report.

> **FINDING 3:** There is no evidence that President Trump agreed with rioters chanting "hang Mike Pence."

The Select Committee—relying on nothing other than Hutchinson's testimony—incorrectly asserted in its Report that President Trump agreed with the rioters chanting that Vice President Pence deserved to be hanged.[123] From the Select Committee Report:

> Evidence developed in the Committee's investigation showed that the President, when told that the crowd was chanting "Hang Mike Pence," responded that perhaps the Vice President deserved to be hanged.[642]

[124]

Cassidy Hutchinson presented an evolving account of the claim that President Trump supported the idea that Vice President Pence deserved to be hanged. Initially, Hutchinson failed to mention this allegation—or anything at all related to hangings—in either her February 23, 2022, or March 7, 2022, interviews with the Select Committee.[125] It was not until her May 17, 2022, interview that the topic came up at all, and it was at Representative Cheney's insistence.[126]

Cassidy Hutchinson's first narrative of the chanting incident lacks internal cohesion. Hutchinson states that she personally saw and heard Meadows and President Trump discuss the rioters' chants about hanging Vice President Pence, and how Meadows and President Trump "personally felt about it at the time."[127]

---

[123] STAFF OF H. SELECT COMM. TO INVESTIGATE THE JAN. 6TH ATTACK ON THE U.S. CAPITOL, 117TH CONG., FINAL REP. 111 (Comm. Print 2022).

[124] *Id.* (citing Cassidy Hutchinson's Transcribed Interview on May 17, 2022, as its sole source).

[125] Select Comm. to Investigate the Jan. 6th Attack on the U.S. Capitol, Transcribed Interview of Cassidy Hutchinson (Feb. 23, 2022); Select Comm. to Investigate the Jan. 6th Attack on the U.S. Capitol, Transcribed Interview of Cassidy Hutchinson (Mar. 7, 2022).

[126] Select Comm. to Investigate the Jan. 6th Attack on the U.S. Capitol, Transcribed Interview of Cassidy Hutchinson 5-12 (May 17, 2022).

[127] *Id.* at 5.

> Ms. Cheney. Did you hear the President say anything about the chants about hang Mike Pence?
>
> Ms. Hutchinson. He had been aware that that was being chanted at the time.
>
> Ms. Cheney. And did you hear him say anything about that?
>
> Ms. Hutchinson. I heard him kind of question if it was our supporters and how many people there were chanting that at the time. And I had heard Mr. Meadows and him having a conversation about the chants and if there is anything they should do about it or how they personally felt about it at the time.

[128]

However, just a few minutes later in that same interview, Hutchinson claims that she had no firsthand knowledge of President Trump's personal feelings about the chant, having neither seen nor heard him talk about it with Meadows.[129] She states that she could only testify to her "understanding" of the conversation, and that she could not specify President Trump's intent when this alleged conversation took place because she "wasn't there."[130]

> Ms. Hutchinson. Mr. Trump at that time, the way that I understand -- understood it then and understand it now, had said something along those lines, but I don't -- I wasn't there. I didn't hear the tone of voice that he said it in. I don't know if he was being sarcastic or if it was more of a broad blanket statement of him just being very frustrated with Mr. Pence this day. You know, I don't want to attribute anything he said to deliberate actions.

[131]

In fact, the most specific claim Hutchinson makes in that same interview about the alleged conversation between President Trump and Meadows comes from her thirdhand eavesdropping on a conversation between Meadows and two attorneys who worked as White House Counsel and as senior advisors for President Trump, Pasquale "Pat" Cipollone ("Cipollone") and Eric Herschmann ("Herschmann") respectively.[132] Hutchinson attributes her claim that Trump agreed

---

[128] *Id.*
[129] *Id.*
[130] *Id.* at 12.
[131] *Id.*
[132] *Id.* at 11.

with the rioters' chant to her recollection of this conversation.[133] In her words, "Mr. Trump had *hypothetically potentially* said that *maybe perhaps* the chants were justified."[134]

> But I recall Mr. Meadows coming back saying that Mr. Trump had hypothetically potentially said that maybe perhaps the chants were justified, he's not doing the right thing, he's not a true patriot, maybe our supporters have the right idea, and not really adding additional commentary at that point. And the attorneys were very specific in wanting to take action on that at the time when they stepped into Mr. Meadows' office and closed the door.

[135]

The Select Committee took Hutchinson's three conflicting stories of the same incident at face value for their Final Report. This level of indifference to the veracity of Hutchinson's claims permeates the Select Committee's Report and serves to highlight Representative Cheney and the House Democrats' willingness to stretch an idea of an allegation into a full-blown accusation, or in most cases, a foregone conclusion.

Nearly eighteen months after the events of January 6, 2021, and a month after testifying that her recollection was no better than saying President Trump "hypothetically potentially said that maybe perhaps…" he agreed with the rioters' chants, Hutchinson suddenly recalled specific details of the alleged conversation between Meadows, Cipollone, and Herschmann. In Hutchinson's words:

---

[133] *Id.*
[134] *Id.*
[135] *Id.*

> I remember Pat saying something to the effect of, "Mark, we need to do something more. They're literally calling for the Vice President to be F'ing hung."
>
> And Mark had responded something to the effect of, "You heard him, Pat. He thinks Mike deserves it. He doesn't think they're doing anything wrong."
>
> To which Pat said something, "This is F'ing crazy. We need to be doing something more," briefly stepped into Mark's office.
>
> And when Mark had said something -- when Mark had said something to the effect of, "He doesn't think they're doing anything wrong," knowing what I had heard

[136]

It is noteworthy that the drastic change in Hutchinson's story occurred after Representative Cheney directed Hutchinson to fire her attorney and hire counsel that Representative Cheney suggested. Hutchinson did not think this incident was worth mentioning during the first two interviews, nor in conversation with her attorney, nor in conversation with her closest friends.[137]

Unfortunately for Hutchinson and the Select Committee's narrative, Chairman Loudermilk and the Subcommittee recovered the transcript of the Select Committee interview of a White House employee who was near the President for the majority of January 6, 2021, and who reliably testified to the President's actions throughout this specific period of time.[138] His eyewitness testimony directly contradicts Hutchinson's third-hand account. In his words:[139]

19	Q We understand that during the events at the Capitol, there were a number
20	of chants, one of which was, "hang Mike Pence."
21	Do you remember any comments that the President or anybody around him made
22	with respect to those chants, "hang Mike Pence"?
23	A No. I remember that happening, but I don't remember any comments
24	from the President or anybody on staff.

[140]

---

[136] *Id.* at 27-28.

[137] Select Comm. to Investigate the Jan. 6th Attack on the U.S. Capitol, Transcribed Interview of Cassidy Hutchinson 109-110 (Sept. 14, 2022).

[138] Select Comm. to Investigate the Jan. 6th Attack on the U.S. Capitol, Transcribed Interview of White House Employee One (redacted) (June 10, 2022).

[139] *Id.*

[140] *Id.* at 42.

This individual was within earshot of President Trump the entire time the President was in the President's Dining Room. Additionally, in its investigation, the Subcommittee spoke with numerous individuals who worked closely with Meadows in the White House, and they confirmed that Meadows would not react apathetically to calls for violence, nor repeat an incident like the one alleged by Hutchinson so carelessly in a public space.

The Select Committee did not thoroughly investigate Hutchinson's allegation against President Trump. The Select Committee only interviewed Herschmann one time on April 6, 2022, and did not ask Herschmann about President Trump's reaction to the chants to "hang Mike Pence."[141] The Select Committee did not re-interview Herschmann to verify Hutchinson's claims. Cipollone, on the other hand, was interviewed on July 8, 2022. He stated that he viewed those chants as "outrageous," and when asked if he recalled a "contrary view" expressed within the White House, Cipollone replied, "I don't have a recollection, a clear recollection, of contrary views on that, personally."[142]

It is clear that the Select Committee relied on Hutchinson's version of events alone, an account based on a conversation that "hypothetically, potentially, maybe perhaps" happened, despite her inconsistent testimony and the overwhelming weight of contrary evidence. Again, Vice Chair Cheney and the Select Committee put narrative over truth.

FINDING 4: Cassidy Hutchinson falsely claimed to have drafted a handwritten note for President Trump on January 6.

Perhaps one of the more bizarre fabrications Cassidy Hutchinson submitted to the Select Committee was her claim that she wrote a note for President Trump relating to the events at the Capitol, when the note clearly was not written by her. While the riot was happening at the Capitol, the Select Committee again tried to portray President Trump as apathetic that the Joint Session had paused due to the violence. This claim was never substantiated by the Select Committee. It appears that Hutchinson took credit for writing a note to President Trump to help bolster the Select Committee's narrative. However, Hutchinson's authorship came under immediate scrutiny following her live public hearing.[143] The Subcommittee retained an independent certified handwriting expert to review the handwriting of the note, and the expert confirmed that Hutchinson's story is not true. While the note in and of itself is not wholly critical to the events of January 6, it demonstrates another example of Hutchinson presenting easily-refutable testimony to the Select Committee, and the Select Committee accepting her fabrications as truth.

---

[141] Select Comm. to Investigate the Jan. 6th Attack on the U.S. Capitol, Transcribed Interview of Eric Herschmann (June 10, 2022).

[142] Select Comm. to Investigate the Jan. 6th Attack on the U.S. Capitol, Transcribed Interview of Pasquale Anthony "Pat" Cipollone 182 (July 8, 2022).

[143] Victor I. Nava, *Former White House lawyer claims Cassidy Hutchinson did not write note to Trump on Jan. 6: Report*, WASH. EXAMINER (June 29, 2022, 5:23 AM).

Cassidy Hutchinson testified at her public hearing on July 28, 2022, that the note in question was written in her handwriting.[144] She claims that Meadows dictated the word "illegally," then attorney Eric Herschmann dictated the words "without proper authority,"[145] and then Hutchinson claims to have written both phrases.[146] This excerpt from Hutchinson's public testimony illustrates her confidence in her claim of authorship:

[144] *On the Jan. 6th Investigation: Hearing before the H. Select Comm. to Investigate the Jan. 6th Attack on the U.S. Capitol*, 117th Cong. (2022).

[145] *Id.*

[146] *Id.*

Ms. Cheney.   Have you seen this note before?

Ms. Hutchinson.   That is a note that I wrote at the direction of the Chief of Staff on January 6th, likely around 3 o'clock.

Ms. Cheney.   And it's written on a Chief of Staff note card.   But that is your handwriting, Ms. Hutchinson?

Ms. Hutchinson.   That is my handwriting.

Ms. Cheney.   And why did you write this note?

Ms. Hutchinson.   The Chief of Staff was in a meeting with Eric Herschmann, potentially Mr. Philbin.   And they had rushed out of the office fairly quickly.   Mark had handed me the note card with one of his pens, and sort of dictating a statement for the President to potentially put out.

Ms. Cheney.   And -- no.   I am sorry.   Go ahead.

Ms. Hutchinson.   No, that is okay.

There were two phrases on there, one illegal and one without properly authority. The illegal phrase was the one that Mr. Meadows had dictated to me.   Mr. Herschmann had chimed in and said also put without legal authority.   There should have been a slash between the two phrases.   It was an "or," if the President had opted to put one of those statements out.   Evidently he didn't.   Later that afternoon, Mark came back from the Oval dining room and put the palm card on my desk with "illegally" crossed out, but said we didn't need to take further action on that statement. [147]

[147] *Id.*

The note in question appears below, written on Chief of Staff letterhead:

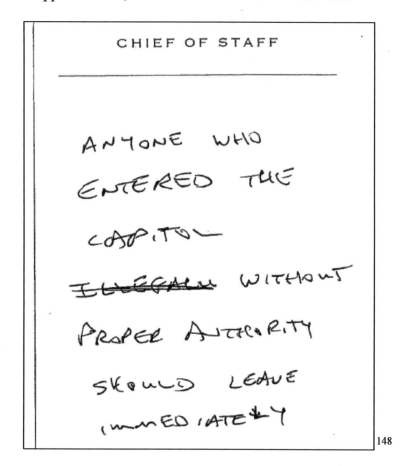

The Select Committee accepted her testimony and accredited Hutchinson with its authorship in its Final Report, based on "[t]he [Select] Committee's review" alone.[149] Immediately following Hutchinson's testimony, however, Herschmann publicly refuted her claim.[150] He has consistently maintained that he is the true author of this note. Inexplicably, the Select Committee did not contact him to confirm, nor did it seek a writing sample for comparison.

[148] KATHERINE KOPPENHAVER, CERTIFIED DOCUMENT EXAMINER, REPORT (July 24, 2024).
[149] STAFF OF H. SELECT COMM. TO INVESTIGATE THE JAN. 6TH ATTACK ON THE U.S. CAPITOL, 117TH CONG., FINAL REP. 79 n.474 (Comm. Print 2022).
[150] John Santucci et al., *Trump White House Attorney disputes Cassidy Hutchinson's testimony about handwritten note*, ABC NEWS (June 28, 2022, 11:07 PM).

Chairman Loudermilk and the Subcommittee obtained a multitude of writing samples from both Hutchinson and Herschmann. First, Hutchinson's sample:

Compared with a few samples of Herschmann's handwriting:

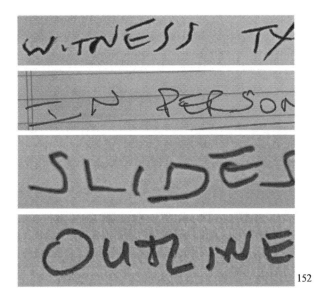

---

[151] Exemplar of Cassidy Hutchinson's handwriting (on file with the Subcommittee).
[152] Exemplars of Eric Hershmann's handwriting (on file with the Subcommittee).

In the interest of identifying the true author, the Subcommittee contracted with an independent certified handwriting expert to verify the note's authorship. The expert conclusively confirmed that the note Hutchinson attested to writing in a public congressional hearing did *not* belong to Hutchinson, but rather that Herschmann authored the note. From the handwriting expert's report: [153]

> **CONCLUSION:**
>
> Based on the documents submitted, the evidence supports my opinion that the handwriting that appears on the Questioned Document was written in the same hand as the exemplars.
>
> [154]

In addition to Hutchinson's dishonesty about this note, it is important to recognize that this is yet another example of the Select Committee relying on evidence it knew, or had reason to know, was untrue. Likely due to Eric Herschmann's passionate pushback against Hutchinson's claims and the visible difference between Hutchinson's handwriting and the note in question, the Select Committee included a footnote in its Final Report stating, "who wrote the note is not material to the Select Committee."[155] Hutchinson testified to a fact that was patently untrue, the Select Committee empowered and promoted her falsehood, and at the end of its investigation, the Select Committee published its Final Report propped up by these unsubstantiated claims.

FINDING 5: President Trump did not have intelligence indicating violence on the morning of January 6.

The Select Committee relied on Hutchinson to make the claim that President Trump ignored briefings from his security team the morning of January 6, 2021, and continued with the plan to hold his rally at the White House Ellipse.[156] However, the Subcommittee has not uncovered any evidence to support this claim. Hutchinson claimed that Tony Ornato told her that he had briefed President Trump about security concerns the morning of January 6.[157] However, in sworn testimony, Ornato expressly refuted Hutchinson's claim and testified that it was not his job to brief the President.[158] Ornato went further to say that he could not have briefed the President on risks of violence, because *he himself* was not aware of any risk of violence on the morning of January 6.[159] In spite of this key contradictory evidence, the Select Committee printed this claim

---

[153] KATHERINE KOPPENHAVER, CERTIFIED DOCUMENT EXAMINER, REPORT (July 24, 2024).

[154] *Id.*

[155] STAFF OF H. SELECT COMM. TO INVESTIGATE THE JAN. 6TH ATTACK ON THE U.S. CAPITOL, 117TH CONG., FINAL REP. 79 n.474 (Comm. Print 2022).

[156] *Id.* at 68-69.

[157] *Id.* at 67.

[158] Select Comm. to Investigate the Jan. 6th Attack on the U.S. Capitol, Transcribed Interview of Anthony Ornato 55 (Nov. 29, 2022).

[159] *Id.* at 55-56.

in its Final Report directly refuted by Ornato, the alleged source, and promoted Hutchinson's account as fact.[160] From the Select Committee's report:

> Testimony indicated that President Trump was briefed on the risk of violence on the morning of the 6th before he left the White House. Cassidy Hutchinson provided this testimony:
>
> Vice Chair Cheney: So, Ms. Hutchinson, is it your understanding that Mr. Ornato told the President about weapons at the rally on the morning of January 6th?
>
> Hutchinson: That is what Mr. Ornato relayed to me.[413]

[161]

Tony Ornato's November 2022 interview with the Select Committee contradicted this claim:

> And I wasn't made aware of anything with weapons prior to the event as far as -- what I recall in all of the reporting from the Secret Service was that there was no civil service disobedience expected from the groups.   So I don't recall that being brought to my attention.

[162]

If the Select Committee sought to investigate and report on the security failures leading up to the events of January 6, 2021, it is unclear why it continued to rely on Hutchinson's unverified allegations. As with the majority of her allegations, the source Hutchinson cited categorically denied the factual basis of her story. President Trump was not briefed on the risk of violence on the morning of January 6, and certainly not by Tony Ornato.

FINDING 6: Cassidy Hutchinson lied about the classification status of documents to disparage Mark Meadows.

In her book, Cassidy Hutchinson claimed that in the final days of the Trump Administration, Mark Meadows gave binders related to Crossfire Hurricane—the codename for the FBI's political investigation into Russian interference in the 2016 election—to a media organization. It

---

[160] *Id.*

[161] STAFF OF H. SELECT COMM. TO INVESTIGATE THE JAN. 6TH ATTACK ON THE U.S. CAPITOL, 117TH CONG., FINAL REP. 46 (Comm. Print 2022).

[162] Select Comm. to Investigate the Jan. 6th Attack on the U.S. Capitol, Transcribed Interview of Anthony Ornato 37 (Nov. 29, 2022).

is worth noting that Crossfire Hurricane, which later became the Mueller Report, concluded that there was no collusion between Russia and the Trump Campaign.[163]

Due to the partisan nature of this investigation, Meadows and President Trump wanted to allow journalists to review the documents associated with this investigation and allow the American public to have access to the truth, and in particular, access to information regarding the actions of certain FBI agents. Meadows cleared the documents for release through all of the appropriate agencies, and only then allowed journalist John Solomon ("Solomon") to review the documents at the White House on January 19, 2021.[164] After this discussion and review of documents, Solomon's staff picked up physical copies of the report that evening to begin the process of scanning and uploading the documents for release.[165] However, in the middle of this scanning operation, the Department of Justice ("DOJ") contacted Meadows, who contacted Solomon, to inform them that it had overlooked a small number of Privacy Act redaction and that the documents needed to be returned.[166] Solomon promptly complied with this request and was told that he would receive an updated copy of the materials before the end of the Administration, at noon on January 20, 2021.[167]

Cassidy Hutchinson's recollection of the event varies significantly from the evidence. Her version, though entirely uncorroborated, states that Meadows gave these documents to Solomon and Mollie Hemmingway, another journalist, while he knew they were still classified.[168] The implication of Hutchinson's account is clear—Meadows, with his extensive experience handling classified information, violated a series of laws to distribute classified information under President Trump's direction, despite the obvious trail that would lead back to himself. Hutchinson's account goes as follows, through her story of a conversation with Deputy Counsel to President Trump Pat Philbin:

---

[163] Report, U.S. DEP'T OF JUST., "Report On The Investigation Into Russian Interference In The 2016 Presidential Election" (Mar. 2019).

[164] Pl.'s Partial Mot. Summ. J., Solomon v. Merrick Garland, et al., at 4, No. 1:23-cv-00759-RJL (D.C. Dist. Ct.).

[165] *Id.* at 5

[166] *Id.* at 6

[167] *Id.*

[168] CASSIDY HUTCHINSON, ENOUGH 234 (2023).

> At around 10:30 p.m., I saw Pat Philbin power walking toward my office. *Great*, I thought. *What could possibly be going wrong now?*
>
> "How many copies of that Crossfire Hurricane binder did Mark make? Where are all the copies?" Pat huffed. "How many of them have been distributed?"
>
> "Slow down," I said to Pat, trying to keep up with his questions, many of which I did not have a response to. "How many copies? I have no idea. There are some in our office..." I glanced around. There were many binders strewn around with still-classified but supposedly soon-to-be-declassified information, but the Crossfire Hurricane binders were easy to identify because of how thick they were.
>
> "Did Mark already give copies to Mollie Hemingway and John Solomon?" Pat asked, referring to the conservative journalists who the president and Mark were acquainted with. I nodded. "Yeah, he had a few of his Secret Service agents meet Mollie and John in Georgetown earlier tonight while you all were in the Oval Office with the boss." The color drained from Pat's face. "Seriously?" he asked. [169]

However, this implication is demonstrably false. On January 19, 2021, President Trump signed a declassification order allowing the Crossfire Hurricane binders to be declassified to the "maximum extent possible."[170] Solomon has stated in court proceedings that he saw the declassification order before reviewing the documents at the White House and has a copy of the order in his possession. See the report in the Federal Register:

---

[169] CASSIDY HUTCHINSON, ENOUGH 234 (2023).

[170] Declassification of Certain Materials Related to the FBI's Crossfire Hurricane Investigation, 86 C.F.R. § 14 (2021).

Federal Register / Vol. 86, No. 14 / Monday, January 25, 2021 / Presidential Documents 6843

Presidential Documents

Memorandum of January 19, 2021

Declassification of Certain Materials Related to the FBI's Crossfire Hurricane Investigation

Memorandum for the Attorney General[,] the Director of National Intelligence[, and] the Director of the Central Intelligence Agency

By the authority vested in me as President by the Constitution and the laws of the United States of America, I hereby direct the following:

Section 1. *Declassification and Release.* At my request, on December 30, 2020, the Department of Justice provided the White House with a binder of materials related to the Federal Bureau of Investigation's Crossfire Hurricane investigation. Portions of the documents in the binder have remained classified and have not been released to the Congress or the public. I requested the documents so that a declassification review could be performed and so I could determine to what extent materials in the binder should be released in unclassified form.

I determined that the materials in that binder should be declassified to the maximum extent possible. In response, and as part of the iterative process of the declassification review, under a cover letter dated January 17, 2021, the Federal Bureau of Investigation noted its continuing objection to any further declassification of the materials in the binder and also, on the basis of a review that included Intelligence Community equities, identified the passages that it believed it was most crucial to keep from public disclosure. I have determined to accept the redactions proposed for continued classification by the FBI in that January 17 submission.

I hereby declassify the remaining materials in the binder. This is my final determination under the declassification review and I have directed the Attorney General to implement the redactions proposed in the FBI's January 17 submission and return to the White House an appropriately redacted copy.

The most likely explanation for Hutchinson's erroneous recollection is that she was ignorant to the facts underlying the classification status of the Crossfire Hurricane documents, and she allowed her perception of the situation to convince her that what she *perceived* to be true about the documents was, in fact, the truth. The Subcommittee was unable to interview Hutchinson and therefore it was unable to identify how many other times Hutchinson in fact testified to events based on her limited, erroneous perception in her sworn testimony.

FINDING 7: Representative Cheney and Cassidy Hutchinson attempted to disbar Stefan Passantino.

After Hutchinson switched attorneys at Representative Cheney's direction, the Select Committee needed to shore up Hutchinson's credibility as a witness and explain away her ever changing testimony. To do this, the Select Committee created a narrative that would make Passantino the scapegoat. They manufactured the story that Passantino gave Hutchinson faulty advice—such as instructing Hutchinson to withhold information, to misrepresent her testimony, and even that Passantino implied he would help Hutchinson with future employment in return for favorable testimony.[171] Contrary to the Select Committee's and Hutchinson's narrative, however, the Subcommittee obtained messages between Alyssa Farah Griffin and Hutchinson where Hutchinson admits that Passantino *was* acting in her best interest and that she agreed with his counsel.[172]

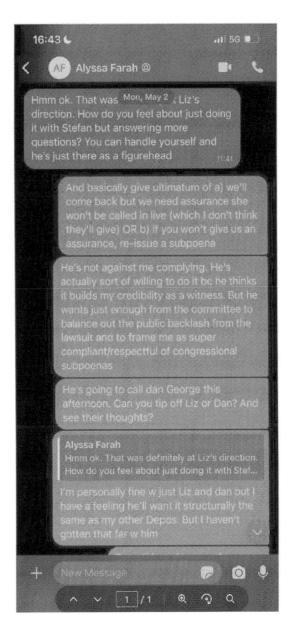

[171] STAFF OF H. SELECT COMM. TO INVESTIGATE THE JAN. 6TH ATTACK ON THE U.S. CAPITOL, 117TH CONG., FINAL REP. (Comm. Print 2022).

[172] Cassidy Hutchinson, private Signal text conversation with Alyssa Farah Griffin (June 6, 2021) (on file with the Subcommittee).

The Subcommittee has reason to believe that the Select Committee coordinated with the Washington, D.C. Bar Association to file an ethics complaint against Passantino. The Select Committee did this by using the content of its not-yet-public report to accuse Passantino of instructing Hutchinson to lie to congressional investigators, sharing information about her testimony with the press over her objections, sharing information about her testimony with other attorneys, and not disclosing who was paying the bill for her representation. This complaint, reviewed by the Subcommittee, was finalized by the D.C. Bar and sent to Passantino the same day the Select Committee's nearly 900-page report was published.

All Bar ethics complaints against Passantino was ultimately dismissed and he was cleared of all of the allegations lodged against him.[173] This episode further demonstrates Hutchinson's willingness to create a false public record that contradicts the truth.

FINDING 8: **Cassidy Hutchinson misrepresented President Trump's actions at Lafayette Square Park in the summer of 2020.**

In addition to Cassidy Hutchison's allegations about the events of January 6, 2021, Hutchinson wrote false statements in her book about the events at Lafayette Square Park on June 1, 2020. In her book, Hutchinson states that President Trump, motivated by his anger, "[ordered] a crackdown" on the Black Lives Matter and Antifa protestors in Lafayette Park prior to visiting historic St. John's Church.[174] The Subcommittee has recovered several interviews performed by the Select Committee that all contradict Hutchinson's version of events.[175]

Cassidy Hutchinson alleged that President Trump ordered law enforcement to clear Lafayette Square Park of protesters. In her words, "the majority of whom were exercising their First Amendment right to free speech."[176]

> On the flight back, the president had expressed his desire that Lafayette Park, across from the White House, the epicenter of the Washington protests, be cleared of the protesters, even the majority of whom were exercising their First Amendment right to free speech, calling attention to social injustices the Black community faces on a daily basis.
>
> [177]

---

[173] Luke Broadwater & Charlie Savage, *Ethics Panels Dismiss Complaints Against Former Lawyer for Jan. 6 Witness*, N.Y. TIMES (Mar. 19, 2024).

[174] CASSIDY HUTCHINSON, ENOUGH 108 (2023).

[175] *See, e.g.*, Select Comm. to Investigate the Jan. 6th Attack on the U.S. Capitol, Transcribed Interview of Robert Engel (Mar. 4, 2022).

[176] CASSIDY HUTCHINSON, ENOUGH 107 (2023).

[177] *Id.*

Her statement contains two important errors. First, many of the protestors in Washington D.C. who occupied Lafayette Square Park had engaged in arson, vandalism, looting, and had assaulted police officers for several days leading up to June 1, 2020.[178] The night before, on May 31, 2020, sixty-one United States Park Police ("USPP") officers and seven D.C. Police officers were injured, with three Park Police officers hospitalized.[179] Two officers were struck by bricks and one required surgery.[180] The protesters who were continually encamped near the walls of the White House in Lafayette Square Park created a hazard to all White House employees and Washington D.C. residents in the area.[181] The violence reached its peak the night of May 31, 2020, and early into the next morning, when protestors set several buildings that border the White House ablaze.[182] St. John's Episcopal Church, which stands directly across Lafayette Square Park from the White House, was set on fire that night as well.[183]

The multi-agency law enforcement response to these attacks was predictable and inevitable, but Hutchinson pushed the false claim that President Trump ordered law enforcement to infringe upon peaceful protester's rights, just so he could give a speech and pose for a photograph.[184]

Cassidy Hutchinson's second baseless claim—that President Trump gave the order to law enforcement to clear Lafayette Square Park for personal gain—was thoroughly debunked by the Department of the Interior Inspector General ("DOI IG").[185] In its report following the law enforcement response to the violent riots at Lafayette Square Park, the DOI IG states the following:

> The evidence we obtained did not support a finding that the USPP cleared the park to allow the President to survey the damage and walk to St. John's Church. Instead, the evidence we reviewed showed that the USPP cleared the park to allow the contractor to safely install the antiscale fencing in response to destruction of property and injury to officers occurring on May 30 and 31.

---

[178] NBC WASHINGTON, *Fires, Looting, Tear Gas: DC in Turmoil Following 3rd Night of Protests* (published May 31, 2020, updated June 1, 2020, 4:04 PM).

[179] *Id.*

[180] *Id.*

[181] Steve Herman, *Violence Erupts Near White House*, VOICE OF AMERICA (May 31, 2020, 2:23 AM).

[182] *Id.*

[183] Peter Herman et al., *Fire set at historic St. John's church during protests of George Floyd's death*, WASH. POST (June 1, 2020).

[184] CASSIDY HUTCHINSON, ENOUGH 108 (2023).

[185] U.S. DEPT. OF INTERIOR OFF. OF INSPECTOR GEN., REVIEW OF U.S. PARK POLICE ACTIONS AT LAFAYETTE PARK (2021).

> Further, the evidence showed that the USPP did not know about the President's potential movement until mid- to late afternoon on June 1—hours after it had begun developing its operational plan and the fencing contractor had arrived in the park. [186]

The report asserts that there is no evidence that USPP cleared the protestors to allow President Trump to make an appearance, and that USPP officers were instead clearing space for contractors to put up fencing in response to the extensive property damage prior to June 1, 2020.[187] Additionally, USPP were not made aware of President Trump's potential movement to the area until hours after USPP's plan was already in action.[188] The DOI IG reaffirmed in its report that USPP retained the authority and discretion necessary to clear the area of any protestors without the need to consult with the White House.[189]

In addition to the DOI IG, Robert Engel, the leader of President Trump's Secret Service detail on June 1, 2020, testified to the Select Committee that there was no discussion of President Trump going to Lafayette Square Park prior to June 1, 2020.[190] He stated that the desire to make an appearance originated the morning of June 1, during President Trump's briefing on the many Black Lives Matter protests across the country.[191]

Cassidy Hutchinson's account in her book represents a false record of the events at Lafayette Square Park. She maliciously attempts to place blame on President Trump for the violent interactions between law enforcement and protestors.[192]

Conclusion

As the Select Committee's star witness, Hutchinson's testimony formed the basis of the Select Committee's false, but most enduring claims against President Trump. Without Hutchinson's altered testimony, it is unlikely the Select Committee could make its assertions about President Trump's mood, attitude, and alleged culpability in the events of January 6. Hutchinson is mentioned by name in the Select Committee's Final Report no fewer than 185 times. Inexplicably, the Select Committee discredited the multitude of legitimate witnesses who, under

---

[186] *Id.* at iii.
[187] *Id.*
[188] *Id.*
[189] *Id.* at 12.
[190] Select Comm. to Investigate the Jan. 6th Attack on the U.S. Capitol, Transcribed Interview of Robert Engel (Mar. 4, 2022).
[191] *Id.*
[192] CASSIDY HUTCHINSON, ENOUGH 107 (2023).

oath, repeatedly refuted Hutchinson's testimony. These legitimate witnesses include senior government officials and federal agents.

As we now know, the Select Committee failed to do its due diligence to verify Hutchinson's radical claims before featuring her testimony on national television during the prime-time slot—going so far as to schedule an emergency hearing to get her claims into public discourse before allowing any credible source to refute them. For example, Hutchinson's story about President Trump reaching for the steering wheel and attacking his Secret Service detail appears for the first time in her fourth interview with the Select Committee on June 20, 2022. Between her fourth interview and her public testimony on June 28—only one week later—the Select Committee did not conduct any on-the-record interviews with the three alleged witnesses who could corroborate this story, instead choosing to rely entirely on Hutchinson's thirdhand account.

According to a profile done on the Select Committee, "[e]ach hearing was preceded by at least two rehearsals held in the Cannon Caucus Room on evenings or weekends. Each monologue was timed with a stopwatch."[193] Every part of the Select Committee's hearings was meticulously planned and executed, except for Hutchinson's. Chair Thompson and Representative Cheney gave the other Members of the Select Committee only three hours' notice before holding Hutchinson's hearing.

The evidence is overwhelming that the Select Committee violated House Rules, deleted documents in the final days of the 117th Congress, and had a predetermined, partisan outcome it was committed to convey—regardless of the facts. The Select Committee's blatant disregard for the truth and Hutchinson's false statements, accepted by the Select Committee as fact, erode all credibility of the Select Committee's Final Report.

Letters

- 1/8/24 Letter from Barry Loudermilk to Cassidy Hutchinson
  - Select Committee Record Preservation and Production Request
- 2/20/24 Letter from Barry Loudermilk to Stefan Passantino
  - Select Committee Record Production Request
- 4/11/24 Letter from Barry Loudermilk to Christopher Wray
  - FBI Interview Records Production Request
- 5/15/24 Letter from Barry Loudermilk to Cassidy Hutchinson
  - Additional Record Production Request
- 5/29/24 Letter from Barry Loudermilk to Colleen Shogan
  - Trump Administration Record Production Request
- 6/4/24 Letter from Barry Loudermilk to Alyssa Farah Griffin
  - Record Production Request
- 6/6/24 Letter from Barry Loudermilk to Fani Willis

---

[193] Robert Draper, et al., *Inside the Jan. 6 Committee*, N.Y. TIMES (Dec. 23, 2023).

- o Communications with Cassidy Hutchinson Inquiry
- 7/1/24 Letter from Barry Loudermilk to Colleen Shogan
  - o Trump Administration Record Production Request

The Select Committee proactively took measures to prevent the public and congressional Republicans from accessing a substantial amount of material in contravention of House Rules.[194] This includes all video recordings of hundreds of interviews, transcripts of several key interviews, and several terabytes of data. In addition to deleting data, the Select Committee effectively concealed many vital interviews from subsequent congressional committees by giving "custody" of those transcripts to the executive agencies like the Department of Homeland Security ("DHS"), and instead of archiving those transcripts with the Clerk of the House as mandated by House Rules,[195] the Select Committee deleted its copies of those transcripts.[196] Because of this decision, it took the Subcommittee several months to recover copies of those transcripts from DHS, and when the documents were finally delivered, they were incomplete and contained significant redactions. The Select Committee's efforts to conceal those records from later congressional review led to predictable and unnecessary delays.

The Subcommittee, in longstanding negotiations with the White House and DHS, recovered seventeen transcribed interview transcripts that the Select Committee failed to archive, in clear violation of House Rules.[197] These transcripts included United States Secret Service Agents and other White House employees. Many of these transcripts directly refute the narrative told by the Select Committee, yet they were never archived. Additionally, the Select Committee did not conduct most of these interviews until November 2022, after Democrats lost their majority in Congress.

These transcripts encompassed agents in proximity to President Trump, Vice President Pence, Chief of Staff Meadows, and the intelligence and operations divisions of the Secret Service. The Subcommittee recovered the following transcripts of interviews conducted by the Select Committee of United States Secret Service Agents:

1) Robert (Bobby) Engel – November 17, 2022, *Special Agent in Charge for POTUS*

2) Robert (Bobby) Engel – March 4, 2022, *Special Agent in Charge for POTUS*

3) John Gutsmeidl – November 2, 2022, *Manpower Assistant Special Agent in Charge for POTUS*

4) Unnamed Agent* – November 4, 2022, *Lead Transportation Agent for POTUS*

5) Unnamed Agent* – November 7, 2022, *Driver of POTUS' SUV*

6) Timothy Giebels – April 8, 2022, *Special Agent in Charge for VPOTUS*

---

[194] *See e.g.*, H.R. Res. 503, 117th Cong. (2021); Letter from Nancy Pelosi, Speaker, H.R., to Bennie Thompson, Chairman, Select Comm. to Investigate the Jan. 6th Attack on the U.S. Capitol (Dec. 29, 2022) (on file with the Subcommittee); H.R. Res. 5, 118th Cong. (2023).
[195] Rule 7, Rules of the H.R., 117th Cong. (2021).
[196] LIZ CHENEY, OATH AND HONOR 357 (2023).
[197] Rule 7, Rules of the H.R., 117th Cong. (2021).

7) Unnamed Agent* – November 21, 2022, *Assistant Detail Leader for COS Meadows*

8) Unnamed Agent* – November 18, 2022, *Assistant Detail Leader for COS Meadows*

9) Tony Ornato – January 28, 2022, *Deputy Chief of Staff for Operations*

10) Tony Ornato – March 29, 2022, *Deputy Chief of Staff for Operations*

11) Tony Ornato – November 29, 2022, *Deputy Chief of Staff for Operations*

12) David Torres – March 2, 2022, *Deputy Assistant Director for Strategic Intelligence*

13) Anthony Guglielmi – October 31, 2022, *USSS Chief of Communications, started 3/2022*

There are four agents who are under GS-14, and therefore their names and certain identifying information will remain redacted to protect their privacy. Their names are not relevant to the role they played on January 6, 2021.

The Subcommittee recovered additional transcripts from the Select Committee's transcribed interviews of White House employees, each of whom will remain anonymous to protect their privacy. These transcribed interviews were released as part of the Subcommittee's Initial Findings Report in March 2024.[198]

1) Unnamed Employee – June 10, 2022, *with direct knowledge of POTUS demeanor and actions*

2) Unnamed Employee – July 11, 2022, *Situation Room Desk Officer*

3) Unnamed Employee – July 18, 2022, *with national security responsibilities*

4) Unnamed Employee – September 12, 2022, *with national security responsibilities*

At the end of every Congress, committees, including select committees, must archive relevant committee materials with the Clerk of the House.[199] These materials include transcripts, exhibits, depositions, communications from stakeholders, press files, reports, research files, document production, executive branch communications, and a number of other materials.[200] The Clerk of the House then holds on to these records for four years before then transmitting them to the National Archives and Records Administration ("NARA").[201]

However, Representative Cheney, in her book *Oath and Honor*, attempts to rewrite history by willfully misrepresenting the role of the Select Committee in archiving these transcripts.

---

[198] STAFF OF COMM. ON H. ADMIN. SUBCOMM. ON OVERSIGHT, 118TH CONG. INITIAL FINDINGS REP. (Comm. Print 2024).

[199] Letter from Bennie Thompson, Chairman, Select Comm. to Investigate the Jan. 6th Attack on the U.S. Capitol, and Liz Cheney, Vice Chair, to Jonathan Meyer (Dec. 30, 2022) (on file with the Subcommittee).

[200] H.R. OFF. OF THE CLERK, Rec. Mgmt. Manual for Comm's. (Sept. 2023).

[201] Letter from Colleen Shogan to Barry Loudermilk, Chairman, Comm. on H. Admin. Oversight Subcomm. (May 30, 2024) (on file with the Subcommittee).

> As we prepared the *Final Report* for publication, we also got ready to release the Committee's interview transcripts. We ultimately released all but a handful.
>
> Only for certain Secret Service, national-security, and military witnesses was the January 6th Select Committee obligated, as a condition for obtaining testimony, to return the transcripts to the government entity involved. In the few cases of this type, the Committee requested that the government entities perform whatever redactions were necessary to safeguard sensitive national-security information, then supply the edited transcripts to the National Archives. [202]

The Select Committee, by asking for the "timely return" of documents, implies that Representative Cheney, who signed the letter to DHS, understood these are House-created documents. Additionally, "designation of instructions for proper handling by the Archives" understands that it is the job of the House to transmit these documents to NARA, not DHS itself.

In yet another example of manipulating the details to paint herself in the best light, Representative Cheney tried to put the onus on DHS to transmit these documents to NARA, yet DHS cannot transmit House documents on behalf of the House. Once again, Representative Cheney demonstrated that she was trying to hide this evidence in the executive branch to prevent it from ever contradicting her predetermined narrative against President Trump. [203]

The Select Committee also used these unarchived transcripts as sources in their final report. The Select Committee touted its research, but it did not release the transcripts that directly refute its narrative. This is indicative of deliberate deception. See below for a citation for one of the missing DHS transcripts: [204]

> 450. Select Committee to Investigate the January 6th Attack on the United States Capitol, Transcribed Interview of United States Secret Service Agent, (Nov. 21, 2022), pp. 22-23. The Select Committee has agreed to keep confidential the identity of this witness due to their sensitive national security responsibilities.

The Select Committee justified releasing some transcripts over others based on inconsistent standards. The Select Committee believed "Mr. Ornato's November 2022 transcript addressed a range of intelligence information important to the Committee's conclusions about January 6th," [205] but did not the transcript of the interview of Secret Service Director of Communications, Anthony Guglielmi ("Guglielmi"). Both Ornato's and the Guglielmi's testimonies contained relatively equivalent levels of "sensitive national-security information," but the likely because

---

[202] LIZ CHENEY, OATH AND HONOR 357 (2023).

[203] *Id.*

[204] STAFF OF H. SELECT COMM. TO INVESTIGATE THE JAN. 6TH ATTACK ON THE U.S. CAPITOL, 117TH CONG., FINAL REP. (Comm. Print 2022).

[205] *Id.*

Guglielmi's testimony refutes Hutchinson's claims much more directly, his interview was never published by the Select Committee. From his testimony:

> A   Mr. Ornato advised me that he was in the West Wing at the time of all this. And he had taken issue with some of the claims of Ms. Hutchinson's testimony -- not the entire testimony.   I think some of it was accurate, but there was a portion of it that was misconstrued, according to Mr. Ornato, that he did not have that conversation, he told me.
>
> Q   Which part of it did he tell you was misconstrued?

> A   He told me he never said that to Ms. Hutchinson.
>
> Q   Never said what?
>
> A   Never had that conversation about the President attempting to assault Bobby Engel.
>
> Q   So Mr. Ornato told you that he never said at any time the President tried to assault Bobby Engel?
>
> A   That's what he told me, yes.   And then we contacted Mr. Engel, and he confirmed to us that the President did not try to physically assault him. [206]

It is also worth considering that the Select Committee may have only released Ornato's November 2022 interview transcript to make it seem like it was Hutchinson's word against Ornato's. In reality, it was the driver, Engel, Ornato, Guglielmi, and the lead transportation agents' collective word against Hutchinson's.

Evidence of Collusion between Special Counsel Jack Smith and President Trump's Adversaries

Chairman Loudermilk and the Subcommittee have uncovered evidence of collusion between the Special Counsel Jack Smith—the prosecutor appointed by Attorney General Merick Garland to conduct two separate criminal investigations into President Trump[207]—and either the White

---

[206] Select Comm. to Investigate the Jan. 6th Attack on the U.S. Capitol, Transcribed Interview of Anthony Guglielmi [p.45] (Oct. 31, 2022).
[207] Press Release, U.S. DEP'T OF JUST., Appointment of a Special Counsel (Nov. 18, 2022).

House or the Select Committee. On October 18, 2024, Special Counsel Smith released some of the documents used in his filing against President Trump.[208]

Among the released documents was an unredacted version of the transcript of a Select Committee interview with a certain White House employee.[209] Given that the Select Committee did not archive, or otherwise destroyed this transcript, and that the White House refused to provide an unredacted version to the Subcommittee, the only remaining explanation is that Special Counsel Smith received the unredacted version from one of the two institutions which did not cooperate fully with the Subcommittee.

Letters
- 8/8/23 Letter from Barry Loudermilk to Jonathan Meyer
  - Select Committee Record Production Request
- 8/8/23 Letter from Barry Loudermilk to White House Counsel
  - Select Committee Record Production Request
- 8/25/23 Letter from Barry Loudermilk to White House Counsel
  - Unredacted Transcript Production Request
- 1/18/24 Letter from Barry Loudermilk to Jonathan Meyer
  - Follow-up Record Production Request
- 1/18/24 Letter from Barry Loudermilk to White House Counsel
  - Unredacted Transcript Production Request

---

[208] April Ruben, *More docs unsealed in Jack Smith's Jan. 6 case against Trump*, AXIOS (Oct. 18, 2024).
[209] Kyle Cheney (@kyledcheney), X (Oct. 18, 2024, 11:45 AM).

In 2022, Home Box Office, Inc. ("HBO") released a documentary film, "Pelosi in the House," focused on the life and career of Speaker Emerita Nancy Pelosi. This documentary film was directed and produced by Alexandra Pelosi, Speaker Pelosi's daughter. The documentary includes footage of Speaker Pelosi and members of House and Senate leadership after being evacuated from the Capitol Complex on January 6, 2021.

The Select Committee was in possession of Alexandra Pelosi's footage throughout their investigation. However, the Select Committee did not publicly release any of the video and furthermore did not archive this footage at the end of the 117th Congress or hand it over when Republicans took the majority in the House of Representatives in 2023.

Despite attempts to conceal the footage, Chairman Loudermilk secured various clips from HBO, containing candid details regarding the events and individuals at the U.S. Capitol on January 6, 2021.

On May 23, 2024, Chairman Loudermilk wrote to HBO, requesting any footage related to the security failures that occurred on January 6, 2021.[210] On June 6, 2024, HBO produced forty-one video files to the Subcommittee. Upon receiving the video production from HBO, Chairman Loudermilk submitted another request for "all raw, unedited footage" from January 6 and January 7.[211] On August 23, 2024, HBO produced twenty-seven additional video files.[212]

The footage, which the Select Committee chose to conceal from public release, contains shocking new information regarding Speaker Pelosi's movements and communication on January 6, 2021.

In one clip, while being evacuated from the Capitol, Speaker Pelosi takes responsibility for the lack of security at the U.S. Capitol. In a very panicked exchange, Speaker Pelosi admits to her Chief of Staff, Terri McCullough, that they bear responsibility for not having adequate security measures established, specifically the National Guard, before the demonstrators breached the Capitol.

---

[210] Letter from Barry Loudermilk, Chairman, Comm. on H. Admin. Oversight Subcomm., to Home Box Office Inc. (May 23, 2024) (on file with the Subcommittee).

[211] Letter from Barry Loudermilk, Chairman, Comm. on H. Admin. Oversight Subcomm., to Home Box Office Inc. (June 25, 2024) (on file with the Subcommittee).

[212] Videotape: HBO Documentary Footage, available at:
https://app.box.com/file/1721600567788?s=8e1dkfi4n19vpwo295j4yqo5mzbc3j3r (on file with the Subcommittee).

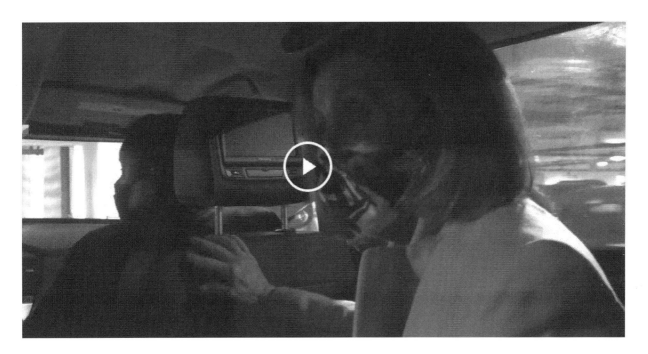

"[Speaker Pelosi]: **We have responsibility Terri. We did not have any accountability for what was going on there; and we should have.** This is ridiculous. You're going to ask me in the middle of the thing [Joint Session of Congress], when they've already breached the inaugural stuff that should we call Capitol Police? **I mean, the National Guard. Why weren't the National Guard there to begin with?**

[Chief of Staff Terri McCullough]: They thought that they had sufficient resources…

[Speaker Pelosi]: No, it's not a question of how they had—they don't know. They clearly didn't know. **And I take responsibility** for not having them just prepare for more."

Prior to January 6, 2021, the U.S. Capitol Police Chief was required by law to receive approval from the Capitol Police Board before directly requesting assistance from the D.C. National Guard.[213] This requirement caused significant delays in the deployment of the National Guard and therefore delayed law enforcement's efforts to secure the Capitol.[214]

[213] STAFF OF S. COMM. ON HOMELAND SEC. AND GOV'T AFF. AND S. COMM. ON RULES AND ADMIN., 117TH CONG., EXAMINING THE U.S. CAPITOL ATTACK, A REVIEW OF THE SECURITY, PLANNING, AND RESPONSE FAILURES ON JAN. 6 (Comm. Print 2022).
[214] Select Comm. to Investigate the Jan. 6th Attack on the U.S. Capitol, Transcribed Interview of Steven Sund 180 (Apr. 20, 2022).

The recorded admission by Speaker Pelosi, outlined above, is only one example of the video footage shot by Alexandra Pelosi which provides new insight into the details of the security failures at the U.S. Capitol and helps to answer the larger question of what happened on January 6, 2021.

Other instances of the HBO footage secured by the Subcommittee throughout its investigation are discussed in other chapters of this report. All HBO video footage obtained by the Subcommittee can be found HERE.

The Committee on House Administration Subcommittee on Oversight ("Subcommittee") has conducted an exhaustive investigation into the Department of Defense's response to the events at the U.S. Capitol on January 6, 2021.

Regrettably, the Select Committee to Investigate the January 6th Attack on the United States Capitol ("Select Committee") only included the National Guard's role in the response as Appendix One to their 845-page Final Report. However, the Subcommittee maintains that the D.C. National Guard delay in quelling the violence at the Capitol is central to understanding the major security failures that occurred on January 6, 2021, as well as adequately responding to an attack of this magnitude in the future.

At 12:53 PM on January 6, 2021, the first breach of the United States Capitol Police ("USCP") perimeter occurred at the West Front of the Capitol.[215] At 2:36 PM, USCP Chief Steven Sund urgently requested National Guard support during a conference call with senior Pentagon officials, city government officials, and D.C. National Guard ("DCNG") senior leadership, including Major General William Walker.[216]

However, the DCNG, also known as the "Capital Guardians,"[217] were not immediately authorized to respond. Although ready to go, the DCNG sat on buses only 1.8 miles from the U.S. Capitol as they waited for the Pentagon to communicate the necessary deployment order. Sadly, Secretary of the Army Ryan McCarthy would not approve the DCNG's movement to the Capitol until after 5:00 PM on January 6, 2021. Two hours and forty-two minutes after USCP's initial request on the 2:30 PM call, 154 D.C. Guardsmen arrived at the Capitol to support USCP at 5:20 PM.[218]

The Subcommittee has uncovered evidence that senior Department of Defense ("DoD") and Pentagon officials were responsible for the **significant and intentional delay** in approving the DCNG deployment to the U.S. Capitol on January 6, 2021, despite directions from the Commander-in-Chief to use military assets to prevent violence.

Furthermore, the Department of Defense Inspector General ("DoD IG") failed to adequately investigate and evaluate the DoD's role in responding to the crisis at the United States Capitol on January 6, 2021. The DoD IG published a flawed report in November 2021, *Review of the DoD's Role, Responsibilities, and Actions to Prepare for and Respond to the Protest and Its Aftermath at the U.S. Capitol Campus on January 6, 2021* ("DoD IG Report"), to construct an inaccurate narrative of the Pentagon's delay on January 6, and therefore permanently alter the historical

---

[215] U.S. CAPITOL POLICE, *Timeline of Events for January 6, 2021 Attack* 11 (2021).

[216] D.C. NAT'L GUARD, *Memorandum for the Rec. from Joint Force Headquarters* 2 (Jan. 7, 2021).

[217] *Heritage,* DISTRICT OF COLUMBIA NATIONAL GUARD (Accessed Nov. 14, 2024).

[218] D.C. NAT'L GUARD, *Memorandum for the Record from Joint Force Headquarters* 4 (Jan. 7, 2021).

record.[219] The DoD IG Report construes a narrative that absolves Pentagon officials of any culpability or wrongdoing and blames the D.C. National Guard for the delay in responding to the Capitol on January 6, 2021. The Subcommittee's investigation was further informed by D.C. National Guardsmen who were heavily involved in the January 6, 2021, response, but were denied a platform to share information by the DoD Inspector General.

The Subcommittee has developed the following findings:

FINDING 1: The Acting Secretary of Defense, Christopher Miller, dismissed President Trump's January 3, 2021, order to use any and all military assets necessary to ensure safety for the planned demonstrations on January 6, 2021.

FINDING 2: The Secretary of the Army, Ryan McCarthy, intentionally delayed the D.C. National Guard response to the U.S. Capitol on January 6, 2021. Although approved by the Secretary of Defense at 3:04 PM, Secretary McCarthy delayed and failed to communicate deployment orders to the commanding general of the D.C. National Guard.

FINDING 3: At 3:18 PM on January 6, 2021, Secretary of the Army, Ryan McCarthy, deliberately deceived congressional leaders by stating that D.C. National Guard was physically moving to the Capitol, with full knowledge these forces had yet to receive any orders. These false statements contributed to decisions made by congressional leaders regarding the security response to the Capitol.

FINDING 4: The Department of Defense Inspector General published a flawed report that contains fabricated information, ignores crucial information, fails to interview key individuals, and appears to have collaborated with DoD to portray a false narrative.

FINDING 5: DoD and DoD IG knowingly and inaccurately placed blame on D.C. National Guard leadership for the delayed DoD response.

FINDING 6: DoD IG was not responsive to the Subcommittee's requests, and, at times, obstructed the Subcommittee's work. The Subcommittee has detected an inappropriately close relationship between the DoD Inspector General and DoD which compromises the Inspector General's ability to conduct objective oversight.

---

[219] Report, U.S. DEP'T OF DEF. OFF. OF INSPECTOR GEN., "Review of the DoD's Role, Responsibilities, and Actions to Prepare for and Respond to the Protest and Its Aftermath at the U.S. Capitol Campus on January 6, 2021" (Nov. 16, 2021).

The District of Columbia National Guard

The DCNG was founded in 1802 by President Thomas Jefferson to defend the newly created capital city.[220] It is comprised of more than 2,700 soldiers and airmen to provide mission-ready personnel in times of war or national emergency.[221]

Unlike the National Guard units in the fifty states and three territories, where deployment authority rests with those jurisdictions, the DCNG maintains a unique Chain of Command. The DCNG is the only National Guard unit that reports directly to the President.[222] However, Executive Order 11485, signed in October 1969, delegates this authority to the Secretary of Defense.[223] This delegation from the President authorizes and directs the Secretary of Defense to "supervise, administer and control" the DCNG.[224] A Secretary of Defense memorandum further delegates operational control of the DCNG to the Secretary of the Army.[225] These delegations were in place on January 6, 2021, and were relied upon by DoD officials to establish a chain of command for the deployment of the DCNG.

On January 6, 2021, Secretary of the Army Ryan McCarthy maintained approval authority for the deployment of the DCNG.

---

[220] D.C. NAT'L GUARD, *About Us* (accessed Oct. 27, 2024).

[221] *Id.*

[222] *Id.*; D.C. CODE § 49-409 (2024) (effective Mar. 1, 1889).

[223] Exec. Order No. 11485, 3 C.F.R. 15411 (Oct. 1, 1969).

[224] *Id.*

[225] SEC'Y OF DEF. MEMORANDUM, SUPERVISION AND CONTROL OF THE NATIONAL GUARD OF THE DISTRICT OF COLUMBIA (Oct. 10, 1969).

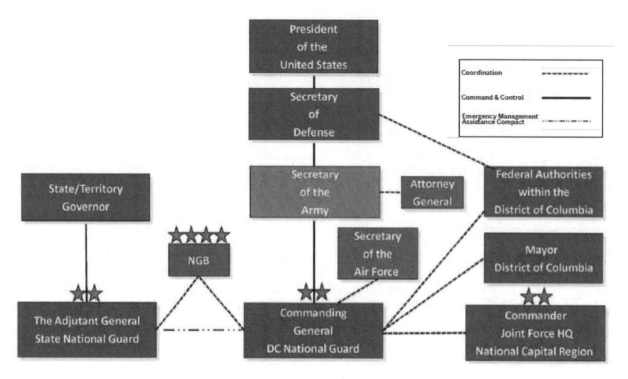

District of Columbia National Guard Command Authority[226]

The DCNG's primary federal and state missions include supporting National Security Significant Events ("NSSE") and civil disturbance across Washington D.C.[227] According to their own website, the DCNG "retains the mission as protector of the District of Columbia."[228] In June 2020, a statement released by the DoD touted the DCNG as the "First Choice in Response to Civil Unrest" and commended them on their response to the major protests across Washington D.C. in the summer of 2020:

"Governors in 28 states have called on the National Guard to support first responders in the wake of civil unrest and protests across the nation following the death of George Floyd.

[226] D.C. NAT'L GUARD, *2019 Annual Report* (2019).
[227] CENTER FOR ARMY LESSONS LEARNED, *Civil Disturbance Operations, District of Columbia National Guard Special Study*, No. 20-579 (2020); D.C. NAT'L GUARD, *About Us* (accessed Oct. 27, 2024).
[228] D.C. NAT'L GUARD, *About Us* (accessed Oct. 27, 2024).

In the U.S., more than 67,000 National Guard soldiers and airmen are supporting operations in every single state, three territories, and the District of Columbia, the official said, noting that this represents the largest domestic response since Hurricane Katrina."[229]

Furthermore, Secretary of the Army Ryan McCarthy was intimately aware of the DCNG's Civil Disturbance capabilities. Prior to January 6, 2021, on May 31, 2020, Secretary McCarthy visited the D.C. Armory to inspect the DCNG alongside Major General Walker and thanked servicemembers for their role in responding to civil disturbance in Washington D.C.[230] Secretary McCarthy also commended the 113th Wing D.C. Air National Guard for their work in June of 2020.[231]

Subcommittee Findings

FINDING 1: The Acting Secretary of Defense, Christopher Miller, dismissed President Trump's January 3, 2021, order to use any and all military assets necessary to ensure safety for the planned demonstrations on January 6, 2021.

On January 3, 2021, Acting Secretary Miller and Chairman of the Joint Chiefs of Staff ("CJCS"), Mark Milley, met with President Trump at the White House.[232] Acting Secretary Miller and Chairman Milley have both testified that, although the purpose of the meeting was unrelated to the events of January 6, President Trump asked both senior Pentagon officials about the safety precautions for the planned demonstrations on January 6, 2021.[233]

The DoD IG interviewed Chairman Milley twice in April of 2021.[234] In his testimony to the DoD IG, Chairman Milley shared specific details of the January 3, 2021, meeting with President Trump:

> "The President just says, **'Hey look at this. It's going to be a large amount of protestors coming here on the 6th, and make sure that you have sufficient National Guard or Soldiers to make sure it's a safe event.'** And [Acting Secretary of Defense] Miller responds by saying, **'Hey, we've got a plan, and we've got it covered.'** And that's about it."[235]

Chairman Milley revealed to the DoD IG that in the January 3, 2021, meeting, President Trump gave the order **"to make sure it's a safe event"** when referring to the planned demonstrations on

---

[229] David Vergun, U.S. DEP'T OF DEF., *DOD Official: National Guard is First Choice in Response to Civil Unrest* (June 3, 2020).

[230] Facebook post, D.C. National Guard, FACEBOOK (May 31, 2020).

[231] Facebook post, 113th Wing D.C. Air National Guard, FACEBOOK (June 5, 2020).

[232] OFF. OF SEC'Y DEF, *Memorandum for the Record* (Jan. 7, 2021) (on file with the Subcommittee).

[233] U.S. Dep't of Def. Inspector Gen., Transcribed Interview of Christopher Miller (Mar. 12, 2021); U.S. Dep't of Def. Inspector Gen., Transcribed Interview of Mark Milley (Apr. 8, 2021) (emphasis added).

[234] U.S. Dep't of Def. Inspector Gen., Transcribed Interview of Mark Milley (Apr. 8, 2021); U.S. Dep't of Def. Inspector Gen., Transcribed Interview of Mark Milley (Apr. 16, 2021) (emphasis added).

[235] U.S. Dep't of Def. Inspector Gen., Transcribed Interview of Mark Milley 23 (Apr. 8, 2021) (emphasis added).

January 6, 2021.[236] Acting Secretary Miller replied to President Trump's concerns with **"we've got a plan and we've got it covered."**[237]

Chairman Milley provided further details to the DoD IG, stating, again, that President Trump ordered his top military officials to use any and all military assets to guarantee safety throughout the planned events of January 6, 2021, during the same meeting on January 3, 2021:

> The President said, "I want 10,000 troops." And that led to this whole kind of controversy about Insurrection Act and so on, which ultimately leads to Secretary Esper being fired. In the meeting on the 3rd of January there was no discussion to my recollection, and I'm sitting there and I'm paying close attention to all of this stuff. There was no discussion of 10,000 troops. It was just what I just described which was, **"Hey, I don't care if you use Guard, or Soldiers, active-duty Soldiers, do whatever you have to do. Just make sure it's safe."**[238]

The following day, on January 4, 2021, Acting Secretary Miller approved a request from D.C. Mayor Bowser for National Guard assistance at traffic control points on January 5 - 6, 2021.[239] On January 4, Acting Secretary Miller issued the "Employment Guidance for the District of Columbia National Guard" memorandum ("January 4 memo") to his Secretary of the Army Ryan McCarthy, who is next in the chain of command for the DCNG.[240]

Acting Secretary Miller's January 4 memo established significant restrictions and control measures for the DCNG and its deployment, requested by Mayor Bowser, on January 5 – 6, 2021:

---

[236] *Id.* (emphasis added).

[237] *Id.* (emphasis added).

[238] U.S. Dep't of Def. Inspector Gen., Transcribed Interview of Mark Milley 23-24 (Apr. 8, 2021) (emphasis added).

[239] Letter from Muriel Bowser, Mayor, Washington, D.C., to William Walker, Major General, D.C. National Guard (Dec. 31, 2020) (on file with the Subcommittee); Letter from Christopher Rodriguez, Doctor, to William Walker, Major General, D.C. National Guard (Dec. 31, 2020) (on file with the Subcommittee).

[240] Memorandum from Christopher Miller, Acting Secretary of Defense, to Ryan McCarthy, Secretary of the Army (Jan. 4, 2021) (on file with the Subcommittee).

SECRETARY OF DEFENSE
1000 DEFENSE PENTAGON
WASHINGTON, DC 20301-1000

JAN - 4 2021

MEMORANDUM FOR SECRETARY OF THE ARMY

SUBJECT: Employment Guidance for the District of Columbia National Guard

This memorandum responds to your January 4, 2021 memorandum regarding the District of Columbia request for District of Columbia National Guard (DCNG) support in response to planned demonstrations from January 5-6, 2021. You are authorized to approve the requested support, subject to my guidance below and subject to consultation with the Attorney General, as required by Executive Order 11485.

Without my subsequent, personal authorization, the DCNG is not authorized the following:

• To be issued weapons, ammunition, bayonets, batons, or ballistic protection equipment such as helmets and body armor.

• To interact physically with protestors, except when necessary in self-defense or defense of others, consistent with the DCNG Rules for the Use of Force.

• To employ any riot control agents.

• To share equipment with law enforcement agencies.

• To use Intelligence, Surveillance, and Reconnaissance (ISR) assets or to conduct ISR or Incident, Awareness, and Assessment activities.

• To employ helicopters or any other air assets.

• To conduct searches, seizures, arrests, or other similar direct law enforcement activity.

• To seek support from any non-DCNG National Guard units.

At all times, the DCNG will remain under the operational and administrative command and control of the Commanding General of the DCNG, who reports to the Secretary of Defense through the Secretary of the Army.

You may employ the DCNG Quick Reaction Force (QRF) only as a last resort and in response to a request from an appropriate civil authority. If the QRF is so employed, DCNG personnel will be clearly marked and/or distinguished from civilian law enforcement personnel, and you will notify me immediately upon your authorization.

Christopher C. Miller
Acting

• "Without my subsequent, personal approval authorization, the DCNG is not authorized the following:

• To be issued weapons, ammunition, bayonets, batons, or ballistic protection equipment such as helmets or body armor.

• To interact physically with protestors, except, when necessary, in self -defense or defense of others, consistent with the DCNG Rules for the Use of Force.

• To employ any riot control agents.

• To share equipment with law enforcement agencies.

• To use Intelligence, Surveillance and Reconnaissance (ISR) assets or to conduct ISR or Incident, Awareness and Assessment activities.

• To employ helicopters or any other air assets.

• To conduct searches or seizures, arrests, or other similar direct law enforcement activity.

- To seek support from any non-DCNG National Guard units."[241]

Acting Secretary Miller published his January 4 memo to approve use of the National Guard the day after his January 3 meeting with President Trump in the Oval office, where in response to the Commander-in-Chief's directive to **"use Guard, or Soldiers, active-duty Soldiers, do whatever you have to do. Just make sure it's [January 6] safe"** replies **"we've got a plan, and we've got it covered."**

On March 12, 2021, the DoD IG interviewed Acting Secretary Miller.[242] Acting Secretary Miller was asked by the DoD IG if he ever thought that **"oh, DoD might need to do something at the Capitol"** in the days leading up to January 6, and Acting Secretary Miller responded that the **"operational plan was this, let's take the D.C. National Guard, keep them away from the Capitol."**[243]. His testimony to the DoD IG indicates that he ignored and dismissed the Commander-in-Chief's order to use any military assets necessary to make sure January 6, 2021, is a **"safe event."**[244]

Acting Secretary Miller further stated to the DoD IG: **"There was absolutely—there is absolutely no way I was putting U.S. Military forces at the Capitol"**[245] as he was concerned it may provoke **"the greatest Constitutional crisis probably since the Civil War."**[246]

Acting Secretary Miller's statements reveal that his decision-making rationale for deploying the DCNG was influenced by media stories suggesting that he was a **"Trump crony."**[247] He was also concerned about online narratives in **"the Twitter sphere,"**[248] as opposed to following orders from the Commander-in-Chief. Miller testifies to DoD IG:

> Then you had this constant drumbeat of, remember when I came in the story was that I was a stuffed suit that I was a **Trump crony** that was going to use the United States Military to conduct a military coup to overthrow the Government, the elected Government of the United States. So that is what was out there in the **Twitter sphere.**[249]

---

[241] *Id.*

[242] U.S. Dep't of Def. Inspector Gen., Transcribed Interview of Christopher Miller (Mar. 12, 2021).

[243] *Id.* at 12 (emphasis added).

[244] U.S. Dep't of Def. Inspector Gen., Transcribed Interview of Mark Milley 23 (Apr. 8, 2021) (emphasis added).

[245] U.S. Dep't of Def. Inspector Gen., Transcribed Interview of Christopher Miller 10 (Mar. 12, 2021) (emphasis added).

[246] *Id.* at 11 (emphasis added).

[247] *Id.* at 10 (emphasis added).

[248] *Id.* (emphasis added).

[249] *Id.* (emphasis added).

I knew if the morning of the 6th or prior if we put U.S. military personnel on the Capitol I would have created, go ahead, **the greatest Constitutional crisis probably since the Civil War**.[250]

Furthermore, on January 3, 2021, Representative Cheney, who would become the Vice Chair of the Select Committee, orchestrated a Washington Post Op-Ed which was signed by all ten living former Secretaries of Defense.[251] Acting Secretary Miller would cite this article as another variable in his decision-making process for approval of the D.C. National Guard:

> . . . 10 former secretaries of Defense whatever week that was before write a letter to the Washington Post, basically a letter to those of us in the Department of Defense cautioning that they were concerned that we were—I was going to use the United State military in a way antithetical to the Constitution. So, we had those elements going on.[252]

On January 14, 2022, Acting Secretary Miller was interviewed again by the Select Committee.[253] When asked about the January 3, 2021, meeting at the White House, Miller dismissed President Trump's concerns as "President Trump banter" and refers to President Trump's comments as "throwaway lines."[254]

> [January 6 Select Committee]: But did he [President Trump] stay out of it in these meetings with you? Did he raise the issue [January 6th demonstrations] with you?
>
> [Acting Secretary of Defense Chris Miller]: Oh, the President's the President. He probably had some **throw away lines**, but nothing, you know, beyond **banter** [...] it was just throwaway comments.[255]

> [Acting Secretary of Defense Chris Miller]: I interpreted it as a bit of presidential banter or President Trump banter that you are all familiar with, and in no way, shape, or form did I interpret that as an order or direction.[256]

The above statements from Acting Secretary of Defense Chris Miller to the DoD IG and the Select Committee reveal that President Trump instructed the highest-ranking Pentagon official to use any and all military assets to ensure safety three days prior to January 6, 2021. The Acting Secretary of Defense concedes that external variables, such as the "Twitter sphere", accusations

---

[250] *Id.* (emphasis added).

[251] Susan B. Glasser, *Forced to Choose between Trump's "Big Lie" and Liz Cheney, the House G.O.P. Chooses the Lie*, NEW YORKER (May 6, 2021); William S. Cohen et al., *Opinion: 10 Former Defense Secretaries: Involving the Military in Election Disputes Would Cross into Dangerous Territory*, WASH. POST (Jan. 3, 2021).

[252] U.S. Dep't of Def. Inspector Gen., Transcribed Interview of Christopher Miller 10-11 (Mar. 12, 2021).

[253] Select Comm. to Investigate the Jan. 6th Attack on the U.S. Capitol, Transcribed Interview of Christopher Miller (Jan. 14, 2022).

[254] *Id.* at 98.

[255] *Id.* at 98-99 (emphasis added).

[256] *Id.* at 99

of being a "Trump crony" and Representative Cheney's Op-Ed, weighed on his mind as he determined how and whether to employ the National Guard on January 6, 2021. During this period of time, Acting Secretary Miller published his January 4 memo, with significant restrictions and control measures on the DCNG.

To date, no investigation or disciplinary action has taken place against Acting Secretary of Defense Miller for his failure to follow directives from the sitting Commander-in-Chief on January 3, 2021.

In fact, the DoD IG Report concludes that that "the decisions made by Mr. Miller [Acting Secretary of Defense]" and "actions taken by the DoD in response to the civil disturbance at the U.S. Capitol Campus on January 6, 2021, **were reasonable in light of the circumstances**."[257] The DoD IG Report also "looked for a role or responsibility for the DoD to act preemptively to prevent or deter what later happened at the Capitol. We found none."[258] The "independent watchdog" failed to examine or consider the January 3, 2021, directives from President Trump— which Acting Secretary of Defense Miller and Chairman Milley confirmed, in sworn testimony—as adequate evidence that DoD should have played a role in preventing the breach of the Capitol Building on January 6, 2021.

FINDING 2: The Secretary of the Army, Ryan McCarthy, intentionally delayed the D.C. National Guard response to the U.S. Capitol on January 6, 2021. Although approved by the Secretary of Defense at 3:04 PM, Secretary McCarthy delayed and failed to communicate deployment orders to the commanding general of the D.C. National Guard.

After Acting Secretary of Defense Miller gave approval to employ the DCNG via his January 4 memo, Secretary of the Army McCarthy conveyed the approval down the chain of command to Major General Walker. On January 5, 2021, Secretary of the Army McCarthy authored a memorandum addressed to General Walker which included the same restrictions as Secretary Miller's January 4 memo, such as withholding authorization for DCNG to "be issued weapons, ammunition, bayonets, and batons" and "interact physically with protestors."[259] However, Secretary McCarthy established an additional restriction of withholding employment of a forty-man Quick Reaction Force ("QRF") until a concept of operations plan ("CONOP") is submitted to the Secretary.[260]

> I withhold authority to approve employment of the DCNG Quick Reaction Force (QRF) and will do so only as a last resort, in response to a request from an

---

[257] Report, U.S. DEP'T OF DEF. OFF. OF INSPECTOR GEN., "Review of the DoD's Role, Responsibilities, and Actions to Prepare for and Respond to the Protest and Its Aftermath at the U.S. Capitol Campus on January 6, 2021" 6 (Nov. 16, 2021) (emphasis added).
[258] *Id.*
[259] Memorandum from Ryan McCarthy, Secretary of the Army, to William Walker, Major General, D.C. National Guard (Jan. 5, 2021) (on file with the Subcommittee).
[260] *Id.*

appropriate civil authority. I will require a concept of operation prior to authorizing employment of the QRF. If the QRF is employed, DCNG personnel will be clearly marked and/or distinguished from civilian law enforcement personnel.[261]

Major General Walker, Commanding General of the DCNG on January 6, described these changes in approval authorization and additional control measures as "**unusual**" in his testimony to the Senate Homeland Security and Governmental Affairs and Senate Rules Committees on March 3, 2021:[262]

> The Secretary of the Army's Jan. 5th letter withheld authority for me to employ the Quick Reaction Force. In addition, the Secretary of the Army's memorandum to me required that a concept of operation be submitted to him before any employment of the QRF. I found that requirement to be **unusual** as was the requirement to seek approval to move Guardsmen supporting MPD to move from one traffic control point to another.[263]

Secretary McCarthy included this requirement for "a concept of operation prior to authorizing employment of the QRF" in his January 5 memo, reserving complete control and responsibility for the deployment of the DCNG. [264]

Although Acting Secretary Miller delegated the ability to "employ the DCNG Quick Reaction Force" down the chain of command, Secretary McCarthy did not delegate this responsibility to Major General Walker. Secretary McCarthy withheld this authority from Major General Walker to deploy his D.C. Guardsmen, including the QRF. These changes in approval authorization and

---

[261] *Id.*

[262] *Examining the U.S. Capitol Attack – Part II: Joint Hearing Before the S. Comm. on Homeland Sec. & Governmental Affs and the S. Comm. on Rules & Admin.*, 117th Cong. (2021) (written testimony of William Walker) (emphasis added).

[263] *Id.*

[264] Memorandum from Ryan McCarthy, Secretary of the Army, to William Walker, Major General, D.C. National Guard (Jan. 5, 2021) (on file with the Subcommittee).

additional restrictions imposed on the DCNG limited their ability to respond rapidly to an emergency at the Capitol on January 6.[265]

SECRETARY OF THE ARMY
WASHINGTON

0 5 JAN 2021

Major General William J. Walker
Commanding General
District of Columbia National Guard
2001 East Capitol Street SE
Washington, DC 20003-1719

Dear General Walker:

    This responds to your letter dated January 1, 2021 recommending approval of the request of Mr. Christopher Rodriguez, Director of District of Columbia Homeland Security and Emergency Management Agency (DCHSEMA), on behalf of the District of Columbia Fire and Emergency Service (DCFEMS) and DC Metropolitan Police Department (MPD) dated December 31, 2020, requesting the District of Columbia National Guard (DCNG) 33rd Civil Support Team (CST) and traffic management and crowd control for planned demonstrations in DC from 5-7 January 2021.

Support to the Civil Authorities of the District of Columbia

    DCHSEMA requested that the DCNG CST conduct the following tasks, upon request, for each event: (1) Chemical, Biological, Radiological, and Nuclear (CBRN) monitoring and hazardous material (HAZMAT) on-site support; (2) liaisons at all required locations; (3) technical decontamination support (on call);[1] (4) Analytical Laboratory Suite (ALS) support (on call); and (5) CST operations and communications capability support. The CST personnel will be partnered with personnel from DCFEMS throughout the course of these missions and will serve solely in a support role to emergency fire and medical first responders.

    DCHSEMA also requested six crowd management teams at specified Metro stations and to prevent overcrowding on Metro platforms; and teams to assist at 30 designated traffic posts.

    Your mission analysis determined that the DCNG could provide all of the requested support. I approve the DCNG to support the MPD with 340 total personnel. DCNG Disposition will include:

    a. Traffic Control Points: 90 personnel (180 total/2 shifts) operating in non-tactical vehicles

    b. Metro station support: 24 personnel (48 total/2 shifts)

---

[1] The requested technical decontamination support will be limited to first responders working with the CST. It will not include the mass decontamination of civilians.

-3-

    I withhold authority to approve employment of the DCNG Quick Reaction Force (QRF) and will do so only as a last resort, in response to a request from an appropriate civil authority. I will require a concept of operation prior to authorizing employment of the QRF. If the QRF is employed, DCNG personnel will be clearly marked and/or distinguished from civilian law enforcement personnel. You will notify me immediately of any requests for QFR employment.

    The support mission for the CST will begin at approximately 0700 hours on January 5, 2021, and will end on January 7, 2021 when DCHSEMA, in coordination with DCFEMS, determines that the mission is complete. Finally, your mission analysis determined that the requested support constitutes valid military training; is within the current capabilities of the DCNG, and will not detract from the readiness of the DCNG.

Approval

    Pursuant to my request, the Deputy Attorney General reviewed and concurred with your plan for support to the civil authorities of the District of Columbia.

    All DCNG personnel associated with this support mission will serve under the provisions of Title 32, U.S.C., Section 502(f). They will serve solely in a support role to the named civil authorities and remain under the command and control of DCNG leadership at all times. DCNG will not be armed for this event however, MPD requests that DCNG members be equipped with safety vests and lighted traffic wands to assist with this mission. Further, MPD requests DCNG personnel supporting the mission be appointed as "Special Police" pursuant to D.C. Code § 5-129.03. They will not engage in the domestic surveillance of U.S. persons.

Ryan D. McCarthy

Moreover, the DoD's pre-January 6, 2021, restrictions—which modified approval authorities—counter the spirit and intent of long-established DoD Defense Support for Civil Authorities ("DCSA") directives.[266]

The DoD's DCSA Directive 3025.18 explicitly states that under **immediate response authority**:

> In response to a request for assistance from a civil authority, under imminently serious conditions and if the time does not permit approval from higher authority, DoD officials may provide an immediate response by temporarily employing the resources under their control, subject to any supplemental direction provided by higher headquarters, to save lives, prevent human suffering, or mitigate great property damage within the United States.[267]

---

[265] *Id.*

[266] U.S. DEP'T OF DEF., Dir. 3025.18, *Defense Support of Civil Authorities (DSCA)* (Dec. 29, 2010).

[267] *Id.* (emphasis added).

The DoD's DCSA Directive 3025.18 explicitly states that under **emergency response authority:**

> In these circumstances, those Federal military commanders have the authority, in extraordinary emergency circumstances where prior authorization by the President is impossible and duly constituted local authorities are unable to control the situation, to engage temporarily in activities that are necessary to quell large-scale, unexpected civil disturbances.[268]

Therefore, according to DoD's own policies, DCNG would ordinarily have the ability to rapidly respond to the "large-scale, unexpected civil disturbance" at the Capitol on January 6—but this ability was explicitly removed by the Acting Secretary of Defense and the Secretary of the Army with the January 4 and January 5 memos.[269] These actions taken by Pentagon leadership led to the DoD's paralysis in response to the riot at the U.S. Capitol.

The Subcommittee concludes that these explicit control measures on the National Guard stem from both ill-advised, poor judgement by the Acting Secretary of Defense and the Secretary of the Army, and DoD leadership's intent to prevent or limit the National Guard's ability to act on January 6.

Furthermore, at approximately 2:30 PM, during a teleconference with Pentagon officials and D.C. government officials, U.S. Capitol Police Chief Sund urgently requested National Guard support.[270] This call represented a verbal and urgent Request for Assistance ("RFA") from the USCP to the Pentagon. Although the purpose of the 2:30 PM call was to request the immediate support of the DCNG, Secretary McCarthy, whose permission was expressly required, **declined to make himself available for the call**. Participants on this call shockingly heard Secretary McCarthy's senior army staff, Lieutenant General Piatt and Major General Flynn, recommend **denying** the request for support displaying a preoccupation with "optics."[271]

Despite the recommendation from Army leadership on this call to deny USCP's urgent RFA, Acting Secretary Miller approved and verbally communicated the RFA approval to Secretary McCarthy at 3:04 PM.[272] Despite this approval, Secretary McCarthy failed to communicate the approval to DCNG.[273] The failure to communicate the order in a timely manner has **never been addressed** by either DoD or oversight bodies, including the Select Committee. The approval to deploy the DCNG was finally communicated "in passing" at 5:08 PM by Army Chief of Staff

---

[268] *Id.* (emphasis added).

[269] Memorandum from Christopher Miller, Acting Secretary of Defense, to Ryan McCarthy, Secretary of the Army, (Jan. 4, 2021) (on file with the Subcommittee); Letter from Ryan McCarthy, Secretary of the Army, to William Walker, Major General, D.C. National Guard (Jan. 5, 2021) (on file with the Subcommittee).

[270] U.S. Capitol Police, *Timeline of Events for January 6, 2021 Attack* 17 (2021).

[271] Memorandum from Earl G. Matthews, *The Harder Right: An Analysis of a Recent DoD Inspector General Investigation and Other Matters* (Dec. 1, 2021); U.S. Dep't of Def. Inspector Gen., Transcribed Interview of Walter Piatt, p. 36 (Mar. 4, 2021) (emphasis added).

[272] OFF. OF SEC'Y DEF., Memorandum for the Record (Jan. 7, 2021) (on file with the Subcommittee).

[273] U.S. Dep't of Def. Inspector Gen., Transcribed Interview of James McConville (Mar. 26, 2021).

James McConville when he observed that Major General Walker remained on the teleconference waiting for direction.[274]

The Subcommittee has concluded that the reason for the delay was Secretary McCarthy's requirement for a CONOP. The CONOP requirement was inserted into Secretary McCarthy's January 5 memo solely for DoD officials to control and restrict the timing and use of the DCNG.[275] While the CONOP was for the DCNG to support the USCP, neither entity was involved in the development. Additionally, DoD never produced a copy of the CONOP nor was it ever seen by anyone to this day. The Subcommittee's found that an actual CONOP was never developed and was never communicated nor disseminated to anyone, demonstrating that the CONOP was never needed.

DoD IG interviews of senior DoD officials indicate that the CONOP requirement for DCNG action was added because the Army was not familiar with the DCNG civil disturbance mission and capability. However, between May and September 2020, Secretary McCarthy received several briefings from DCNG leadership regarding DCNG capabilities and preparedness specifically for civil disturbances and witnessed the execution during the Summer of 2020. Secretary McCarthy also witnessed DCNG rehearsals on Civil Disturbance operations.[276] Clearly, Secretary McCarthy knew the capabilities of the DCNG.

At 3:48 PM on January 6, Secretary McCarthy left the Pentagon and drove to the Metropolitan Police Department's ("MPD") headquarters to meet with Mayor Bowser and "draft the CONOP."[277] The fact that Secretary McCarthy went to MPD instead of USCP or DCNG's command centers illustrated that detailed planning of DCNG deployment was not needed. The Army's only requirement in responding to the USCP RFA was to provide the forces to the USCP as rapidly as possible.[278] If Secretary McCarthy wanted to be involved in the planning and employment of DCNG, he would have traveled to either the DCNG Command Center at the D.C. Armory or the USCP Command Center in accordance with the RFA. Relocating to MPD and claiming to produce a CONOP, without the involvement of either the DCNG or the USCP, is inconsistent with appropriate military planning.

The Subcommittee consulted DoD experts on the addition of the planning requirements days before January 6. It is the opinion of the Subcommittee, and these experts, that the requirement

---

[274] *Id.* (emphasis added).

[275] Letter from Ryan McCarthy, Secretary of the Army, to William Walker, Major General, D.C. National Guard (Jan. 5, 2021) (on file with the Subcommittee).

[276] Facebook post, D.C. National Guard, FACEBOOK (May. 31, 2020).

[277] *Memorandum for the Record from the office of the Secretary of Defense*, p. 2 (Jan. 7, 2021) (on file with the Subcommittee).

[278] U.S. Dep't of Def. Inspector Gen., Transcribed Interview of Steven Sund 31-35 (Mar. 15, 2021).

for a CONOP during the riot was an unreasonable burden and limited the DCNG's quick reaction capability.[279]

To date, no investigation or disciplinary action has taken place against Secretary of the Army Ryan McCarthy for his failure to relay the Acting Secretary of Defense's lawful deployment order at 3:04 PM on January 6, 2021.

FINDING 3: At 3:18 PM on January 6, 2021, Secretary of the Army, Ryan McCarthy, deliberately deceived congressional leaders by stating that D.C National Guard was physically moving to the Capitol, with full knowledge these forces had yet to receive any orders. These false statements contributed to decisions made by congressional leaders regarding the security response to the Capitol.

In June 2024, the Subcommittee obtained unreleased video footage of January 6, 2021, from Home Box Office, Inc. ("HBO"). This was footage that was previously in possession of the Select Committee but was not archived with the House of Representatives. The failure of the Select Committee Chair Bennie Thompson to archive this footage was in violation of House Rule 7 which required the Select Committee to archive all noncurrent records[280] and H.Res. 503 that required the transfer of all records of the Select Committee to the committee designated by the Speaker.[281] However, after months of negotiations with HBO and their parent company Warner Brothers, Chairman Loudermilk obtained some of this footage.[282]

A short video clip shows Speaker Nancy Pelosi, Senate Majority Leader Chuck Schumer and House Majority Leader Steny Hoyer, speaking to Secretary McCarthy at 3:18 PM on January 6, 2021, by phone.[283] While on the call with Secretary McCarthy, Leader Hoyer details the severity of the violence at the Capitol, stating: "there's a critical situation, and a risk of loss of life." Senate Leader Schumer adds: "we have some Senators who are still in their hideaways, they need massive personnel now—can you get Maryland National Guard to come too?"

As the elected officials implored the Secretary of the Army to provide "any and all" support immediately, [284] Secretary McCarthy deceivingly stated that National Guard forces are moving to the Capitol to respond.[285] Speaker Pelosi informed Secretary McCarthy that she is going to call

---

[279] Committee Consultant Contract Agreement Pursuant to 2 U.S.C. § 4301, 5 Stones Intelligence, Inc. (June 3, 2024) (on file with the Subcommittee).
[280] Rule 7, Rules of the H.R., 117th Cong. (2021).
[281] H.R. Res. 503, 117th Cong. (2021).
[282] Letter from Barry Loudermilk, Chairman, Comm. on H. Admin. Oversight Subcomm., to Home Box Office Inc. (June 25, 2024) (on file with the Subcommittee).
[283] Videotape: HBO Documentary Footage, IMG_1782.mp4, available at: https://app.box.com/file/1721600567788?s=8e1dkfi4n19vpwo295j4yqo5mzbc3j3r, (on file with the Subcommittee). (on file with the Subcommittee); Reel 2041 – Source File Metadata Summary Sheet.pdf (on file with the Subcommittee).
[284] Videotape: HBO Documentary Footage, IMG_1782.mp4 (on file with the Subcommittee).
[285] *Id.*

District of Columbia Mayor Muriel Bowser to "share the good news" that he is no longer blocking deployment of the DCNG.[286] Secretary McCarthy quickly replies: "Speaker, I never said no. I just had to get permission. It's not my personal authority. I had to talk to my boss [Secretary of Defense Chris Miller]."[287] Speaker Pelosi asked, "Did you talk to your boss?" to which Secretary McCarthy responded, "I did, yes. We have the green light. We [DCNG] are moving."[288]

This footage contradicts Secretary McCarthy's own official timeline, as well as the official timelines published by the DoD and the DCNG, which each indicate that the DCNG were not notified to deploy to the Capitol until after 5:00 PM.[289] Secretary McCarthy gave the impression to congressional leaders that military forces were physically on their way when he stated "We

---

[286] Id.

[287] Videotape: HBO Documentary Footage, IMG_1782.mp4 (on file with the Subcommittee).

[288] Id.

[289] D.C. NAT'L GUARD, Memorandum for the Record from Joint Force Headquarters (Jan. 7, 2021); Memorandum for the Record from the Secretary of the Army (Jan. 7, 2021); Memorandum for the Record from the office of the Secretary of Defense (Jan. 7, 2021) (on file with the Subcommittee).

[DCNG] are moving." In actuality, the DCNG were positioned at the D.C. Armory, waiting for authorization from Secretary McCarthy to deploy to the U.S. Capitol. The most troubling aspect of these misleading statements is that congressional leaders made decisions affecting the security of Members of Congress and their staff, based on the information that the DCNG was enroute to the Capitol at 3:18 PM.

To date, no investigation or disciplinary action has taken place against Secretary of the Army Ryan McCarthy for deceiving congressional leadership with false statements regarding the delay in deployment of the D.C. National Guard to the U.S. Capitol on January 6, 2021.

> **FINDING 4:** **The Department of Defense Inspector General published a flawed report that contains fabricated information, ignores crucial information, fails to interview key individuals, and appears to have collaborated with DoD to portray a false narrative.**

The DoD IG's investigation into the events of January 6, 2021, failed to uphold the organization's stated values of "independence, integrity, excellence and transparency."[290] The DoD IG report that was commissioned to review DoD actions on January 6, contains errors and omissions that are intrinsically connected to its conclusion, warranting an immediate retraction and correction.

On November 16, 2021, the DoD IG published Report No. 2022-039 ("DoD IG Report"). This report, titled *"Review of the DoD's Role, Responsibilities, and Actions to Prepare for and Respond to the Protest and its Aftermath at the U.S. Capitol Campus on January 6, 2021"*, contains factual inaccuracies and does not conduct any investigative analysis of several substantial events that led to the DoD's delayed response to the riot at the Capitol on January 6, 2021. The report incorrectly absolves senior Army officers of any wrongdoing. Some of the more notable errors include:

- **Withholding Critical Information**

The Subcommittee found that the DoD IG did not publish certain information that would have contradicted the DoD IG Report's final conclusions.

  o **DoD, DoD IG, and the Biden Administration possessed information that exonerated President Trump**. Based on the transcripts provided by the DoD IG to the Subcommittee, Acting Secretary of Defense Miller dismissed an order from President Trump to ensure that the necessary security forces were ready for the events of January 6, 2021, during a meeting several days prior, on January 3, 2021. [see Finding 1].

  o **DoD, DoD IG, and the Biden Administration possessed information that the Secretary of the Army misled senior congressional leaders by stating that the D.C.**

---

[290] U.S. DEP'T OF DEF. INSPECTOR GEN., *Mission and Strategic Plan* (Accessed Nov. 18, 2024).

National Guard was "on the way" with the knowledge that the D.C. National Guard was waiting for an order to deploy. [see Finding 3].

- **Published Misleading Information**

The DoD IG Report overlooks conflicting accounts of critical communications between senior DoD officials, USCP, and DCNG, and lists instances of potential communication as fact—with no evidence that the communications or calls took place.

Specifically, the DoD IG Report suggests that Secretary McCarthy was on the phone with Major General Walker at several points throughout the day on January 6, 2021, despite a lack of any evidence of this. The Subcommittee maintains that these alleged phone calls are **entirely fictional** and were only included in the DoD IG Report to support the Army narrative of events which underpins the Report's conclusion that the DoD's response to January 6 was "appropriate."[291]

The DoD IG Report claims that Secretary McCarthy called Major General Walker at 3:05 PM on January 6, 2021:

> **Mr. McCarthy left Mr. Miller's office and called Major General Walker at approximately 3:05pm.**[292]

This alleged instance of communication between the Secretary of the Army and the Commanding General of the DCNG is a critical detail as both individuals are in the chain of command for approval of DCNG deployment.[293] The Subcommittee has uncovered that at 3:05 PM, Secretary McCarthy had not yet given approval to DCNG Major General Walker to deploy his forces to the U.S. Capitol. Instead, the DCNG remained at the Armory—less than two miles from the Capitol. Army leadership issued the "go-order" order to Major General Walker at 5:08 PM.[294]

Secretary McCarthy did not confirm the claim in any transcribed interview that he "called Major General Walker at approximately 3:05 PM." In his interview with the DoD IG, Secretary

---

[291] Report, U.S. DEP'T OF DEF. INSPECTOR GEN., "Review of the DoD's Role, Responsibilities, and Actions to Prepare for and Respond to the Protest and Its Aftermath at the U.S. Capitol Campus on January 6, 2021," 6 (Nov. 16, 2021) (emphasis added).

[292] *Id.* at 56 (emphasis added).

[293] D.C. CODE § 49-409; Exec. Order No. 11485, 3 C.F.R. 15411 (Oct. 1, 1969); SEC'Y OF DEF. MEMORANDUM, SUPERVISION AND CONTROL OF THE NATIONAL GUARD OF THE DISTRICT OF COLUMBIA (Oct. 10, 1969).

[294] U.S. Dep't of Def. Inspector Gen., Transcribed Interview of James McConville (Mar. 26, 2021).

McCarthy could not recall whether he spoke to Major General Walker at that time, and instead asserts that it was **"one of my [Secretary McCarthy's] immediate staff."**[295]

> [DoD IG] Q: Sir, just to clarify, at 1500 [3:00 PM] hours when it indicates that you directed Major General Walker to begin to prepare to move. **Was it you that were in contact with General Walker, or was it somebody from your office?**
>
> [Secretary McCarthy] A: **I think it was one of my immediate staff** because when I came out there was tremendous, I can't remember exactly if I talked to him about it or if it was my immediate staff.[296]

Unfortunately, the DoD IG did not seek clarification from Secretary McCarthy or press him for specific details to determine whether this critical phone call took place, or who exactly on his staff may have talked to Major General Walker during the phone call.[297]

The Subcommittee formally submitted an inquiry to the DoD IG requesting an explanation and any evidence corroborating the alleged 3:05 PM call.[298] The Subcommittee demanded the DoD IG explain how they could present this information in the Report as fact without Secretary McCarthy positively confirming that he spoke to Major General Walker.[299]

The DoD IG vehemently dismissed the Subcommittee's concerns and provided a lengthy response to explain the statement made in the Report regarding the 3:05 PM phone call. Much to the Subcommittee's dismay, the DoD IG's response did not contain any additional evidence, such as phone records, previously concealed testimony, or video footage to substantiate their claims. According to Major General Walker's testimony, had he received this phone call, the DCNG would have been ready to deploy immediately.[300]

The DoD IG's reply acknowledged that Secretary McCarthy was uncertain if the phone call occurred. The response prefaced that the Secretary of the Army and his immediate staff were operating under a "frenetic pace," and thus, **"As a result, we [DoD IG] are not surprised by the Secretary's lack of certainty about whether he spoke with Major General Walker at 3:05 PM."**[301]

The DoD IG substantiated the 3:05 PM call with statements from their interview with Brigadier General Christopher LaNeve, who, at the time, served as the Director of Operations, Readiness

---

[295] U.S. Dep't of Def. Inspector Gen., Transcribed Interview of Ryan McCarthy 56 (Mar. 18, 2021) (emphasis added).
[296] *Id.* (emphasis added).
[297] *Id.*
[298] Narrative Responses from Dep't of Def. Inspector Gen. (on file with the Subcommittee).
[299] *Id.*
[300] Email from Hillary Lassiter, Deputy Staff Dir., Comm. on H. Admin. Oversight Subcomm., to William Walker, Major General, D.C. National Guard (Aug. 28, 2024) (on file with the Subcommittee).
[301] Narrative Responses from Dep't of Def. Inspector Gen. 4 (emphasis added) (on file with the Subcommittee).

and Mobilization in the Department of the Army Headquarters."[302] In their official response to the Subcommittee, the DoD IG writes:

> Brigadier General LaNeve stated that he and Secretary McCarthy moved out of Secretary Miller's office to a smaller conference room in Secretary Miller's office suite, where Secretary McCarthy **"made some calls."**[303]

However, the DoD IG did not include the entire quote from Brigadier General LaNeve's interview in their response. The entire exchange reveals that Brigadier General LaNeve explicitly stated that he did not know who his boss, Secretary McCarthy, was speaking to on the phone:

> [Brigadier General LaNeve] A: Sir, at one point we moved out of the Acting Secretary's office. We went into a smaller conference room that, it's almost opposite of the hall in his office space there. **The Secretary [of the Army McCarthy] made some calls. At that time I'm not sure exactly who he called at the time.**[304]

> [Brigadier General LaNeve] A: And I believe in one of those phone calls he did talk to General Walker. **Again, I'm not on the phone** and I was making the phone calls with him. But I was around that office space.[305]

The Subcommittee's analysis of this exchange indicates that the DoD IG does not possess any evidence to substantiate the claim that Secretary McCarthy called Major General Walker at 3:05 PM. However, asserting—without evidence—that the phone call did take place, places the blame for the delayed deployment of the DCNG on Major General Walker, and absolves Secretary McCarthy and other Pentagon leadership.

Another example of fabricated information in the DoD IG Report is the claim that Secretary of the Army McCarthy called DCNG Commanding General Walker at 4:35 PM on January 6, 2021, to communicate the deployment order for the National Guard to respond to U.S. Capitol:

> Mr. McCarthy called Major General Walker at approximately 4:35pm and told him that Mr. Miller approved the re-mission request. Mr. McCarthy told Major General Walker to immediately move all available DCNG personnel from the Armory to Lot 16 at the corner of 1st Street and D Street and meet with the MPD Assistant Chief to perform perimeter and clearance operations. After Mr. McCarthy gave Major General Walker the deployment order, he handed the

---

[302] U.S. ARMY GEN. OFF. MGMT. OFF., Biography of Christopher C. LaNeve (accessed on Oct. 10, 2024).

[303] U.S. Dep't of Def. Inspector Gen., Transcribed Interview of Christopher LaNeve 23, 40 (Mar. 3, 2021); Narrative responses from Dep't of Def. Inspector Gen. p. 4 (emphasis added) (on file with the Subcommittee).

[304] U.S. Dep't of Def. Inspector Gen., Transcribed Interview of Christopher LaNeve 23, 40 (Mar. 3, 2021) (emphasis added).

[305] *Id.* (emphasis added).

telephone to Brigadier General LaNeve, who told Major General Walker of the plan's details.[306]

In his interview with the DoD IG on March 18, 2021, Secretary McCarthy asserts that both he and Brigadier General LaNeve spoke to Major General Walker:

> [DoD IG] Q: And who was it that actually spoke to General Walker to give him the order the move?
>
> [Secretary McCarthy] A: I remember being there with General LaNeve. We talked briefly, and then he handled all the specifics.
>
> [DoD IG] Q: When and how did General Walker get the direction to move from the Armory to the Capitol?
>
> [Secretary McCarthy] A: At 16:35 [4:35pm]
>
> [DoD IG] Q: And who from?
>
> [Secretary McCarthy] A: I'm trying to recall if that was -- I was with General LaNeve and we notified him then and then General LaNeve gave the specifics of the link up point, 1st and D, the Assistant Chief Jeff Carol and the specifics, and then it was at that 16:35 [4:35pm].[307]

Secretary McCarthy changed his testimony about the alleged 4:35 PM communication with Major General Walker when interviewed by the Select Committee nearly eleven months later, on February 4, 2022. In his altered testimony to the Select Committee, Secretary McCarthy denied speaking directly to General Walker and testified that it was Brigadier General LaNeve who was the only participant on the alleged phone call, due to the Secretary's preoccupation with preparing talking points for an upcoming press conference with Mayor Bowser.[308]

> [Secretary McCarthy]: we made the call at 4:30, I immediately turned, wrote the talking points down -- **our operations director [Brigadier General LaNeve] made the call. I was worried about my talking points**.[309]

When pressed by the Select Committee as to whether he spoke directly to Major General Walker on the alleged 4:35 PM phone call, Secretary McCarthy confirms that he did not speak, and instead it was Brigadier General LaNeve:

> [Select Committee] Q: It sounds like you did not speak directly to General Walker. Is that fair?

---

[306] Report, U.S. DEP'T OF DEF. OFF. OF INSPECTOR GEN., "Review of the DoD's Role, Responsibilities, and Actions to Prepare for and Respond to the Protest and Its Aftermath at the U.S. Capitol Campus on January 6, 2021" 59-60 (Nov. 16, 2021).

[307] U.S. Dep't of Def. Inspector Gen., Transcribed Interview of Ryan McCarthy 62 (Mar. 18, 2021).

[308] Select Comm. to Investigate the Jan. 6th Attack on the U.S. Capitol, Transcribed Interview of Secretary Ryan McCarthy 130 (Feb. 4, 2022).

[309] *Id.* (emphasis added).

[Secretary McCarthy] A: He was -- the guy who was standing next to me [Brigadier General LaNeve]. Because the moment we finished, they said, we've got to go now, and I had to put my thoughts together in like 2 or 3 minutes, my thoughts together. General LaNeve has the authority to speak as the Secretary of the Army for deployment of capabilities worldwide, so that's not an unusual thing.[310]

In contrast to Secretary McCarthy's testimony, Brigadier General LaNeve denied conveying the verbal authorization to deploy to the Capitol at 4:30 PM to Major General Walker. Brigadier General LaNeve states to the DoD IG that it was Secretary McCarthy who passed on the approval to the DCNG:

[DoD IG] Q: Can I jump back in real quick. This is an important point. So, at 16:32 [4:32pm] there's this verbal authorization. Was it you that passed it on to General Walker or was it Secretary of the --

[Brigadier General LaNeve] A: Yes, sir.

[DoD IG] Q: -- Army that did that?

[Brigadier General LaNeve] A: Sir, Secretary McCarthy I believe passed on that they [DCNG] had the approval.[311]

Brigadier General LaNeve stated to the DoD IG that Secretary McCarthy communicated approval to Major General Walker during the alleged 4:30 PM phone call. However, Secretary McCarthy testified to the Select Committee that **"our operations director [Brigadier General LaNeve] made the call"** because Brigadier General LaNeve **"has the authority to speak as the Secretary of the Army."**[312] Despite the inconsistent testimony, the DoD IG Report has not corrected its false claim that the alleged 4:30 PM phone call occurred.

Major General Walker has consistently denied that he received any communication from Secretary McCarthy or his staff at any point on January 6, 2021, as he was waiting for authorization to deploy his forces to the Capitol. Consistent with testimony from senior Army officials, Major General Walker did not receive approval to leave the D.C. Armory until 5:08 PM on January 6, 2021.[313] This is yet another example of the DoD IG including uncorroborated statements to deflect responsibility for the delayed deployment away from Pentagon officials.

---

[310] Select Comm. to Investigate the Jan. 6th Attack on the U.S. Capitol, Transcribed Interview of Secretary Ryan McCarthy 133 (Feb. 4, 2022).

[311] U.S. Dep't of Def. Inspector Gen., Transcribed Interview of Christopher LaNeve 55 (Mar. 3, 2021).

[312] Select Comm. to Investigate the Jan. 6th Attack on the U.S. Capitol, Transcribed Interview of Ryan McCarthy 130-31 (Feb. 4, 2022) (emphasis added).

[313] U.S. Dep't of Def. Inspector Gen., Transcribed Interview of non-senior Dep't of Def. witness 37-38 (Mar. 23, 2021).

- **Incomplete Witness Selection**

The DoD IG interviewed forty-three witnesses to construct Report 2022-039, however it failed to interview key personnel from the DCNG who were heavily involved in the events of January 6, 2021. The DCNG was pivotal in the DoD response on January 6, and the exclusion of these individuals omits a valuable and necessary perspective.

Major General Walker's senior staff, who were present with the General as the events unfolded at the U.S. Capitol on January 6, 2021, were not interviewed by the DoD IG. These include Adjutant General, Brigadier General Aaron Dean; Staff Judge Advocate, Colonel Earl Matthews; Major General Walker's Aide-de-Camp, First Lieutenant Timothy Nick; Senior Enlisted Advisor, Command Sergeant Major Michael Brooks.[314]

The DoD IG refused to interview any of Major General Walker's senior staff to corroborate their timeline. The Subcommittee raised concerns regarding the incomplete witness list with the DoD IG in an official inquiry.[315] The DoD IG claimed in their replied that **"COL Matthews told our investigators that he was not involved in January 6."**[316] However, the Subcommittee interviewed Colonel Matthews under oath, and he denied this statement.[317] The DoD IG's decision to interview individuals with limited involvement, and not interview the four senior officials with direct firsthand knowledge, introduces more doubt into the objectivity of the DoD IG's Report.

- **Poor Investigate Standards, Failure to Conduct Analysis, and Selectively Published Information and Report Conclusions**

The DoD IG Report is listed as a "Review" instead of an investigation. As such, this Report fails to make any significant attempt to investigate or provide analysis on the impact of DoD decisions or actions.

The interviews conducted by the DoD IG focused on the development and confirmation of the official timeline published by the Army.[318] Most interviews ended abruptly without any detailed questions about the "what and why" pertaining to the events of January 6, 2021.[319]

---

[314] Memorandum from Earl G. Matthews, *The Harder Right: An Analysis of a Recent DoD Inspector General Investigation and Other Matters* (Dec. 1, 2021).

[315] Letter from Barry Loudermilk, Chairman, Comm. on H. Admin. Oversight Subcomm., to Robert Storch, Inspector Gen., Dep't of Def. (Nov. 21, 2024) (on file with the Subcommittee).

[316] Narrative responses from Dep't of Def. Inspector Gen. 3 (emphasis added) (on file with the Subcommittee).

[317] Comm. On H. Admin. Oversight Subcomm., Transcribed Interview of Colonel Earl Matthews (Mar. 6, 2024).

[318] U.S. Dep't of Def. Inspector Gen., Transcribed Interview of Lieutenant General Bryan Fenton (Mar. 24, 2021).

[319] Press Release, COMM. ON H. ADMIN. OVERSIGHT SUBCOMM., New: DoD IG Transcripts Contradict Pentagon January 6 Report, Outline "Optics" Concerns as Reason for DCNG Delay (Sept. 5, 2024).

The DoD IG Report concludes that "the DoD's actions to respond to the USCP's RFA on January 6, 2021, were appropriate, supported by requirements, consistent with the DoD's roles and responsibilities for DSCA, and compliant with laws, regulations, and other applicable guidance."[320] Therefore, the scope of the IG's work merely reviewed whether DoD's actions were "appropriate" and "compliant" and did not include any analysis or investigative rigor.

In fact, during his interview with the DoD IG, Major General Walker raised concern over the DoD IG's scope of investigation:

> [Major General Walker] A: I thought you would ask more about the why. The why. Why did this happen?
>
> [DoD IG] Q: For our review and again this is a review, we're looking at it from a standpoint of, what did DoD do, and how does that conform to current policies, laws, regulations. That's what we're looking at. I think the why that you're hitting -- I think you're getting at is, "Okay, why did this whole thing happen in the first place?" No. that is going to be in someone else's lane.[321]

The Subcommittee has officially requested that the DoD IG publish a corrected report to eliminate all objective inaccuracies in order to preserve a factual historical record of the DoD's actions responding to the U.S. Capitol on January 6, 2021.[322]

5. OTHER ISSUES WITH THE DOD IG REPORT:

The DoD IG Report does not include any of the following information:

- Secretary Miller and Secretary McCarthy's sworn statements indicating that they did not want to deploy the DCNG to the Capitol under any circumstances.[323] These statements were clearly outlined in their transcribed interviews; however, the DoD IG did not include them in its report.

- Pentagon leadership's communication severely limiting the response capability of the DCNG just days before January 6, 2021. These restrictions were unprecedented in their nature, however, the impact of these restrictions on DoD's response was not included or addressed in any way by the DoD IG.

---

[320] Report, U.S. DEP'T OF DEF. OFF. OF INSPECTOR GEN., "Review of the DoD's Role, Responsibilities, and Actions to Prepare for and Respond to the Protest and Its Aftermath at the U.S. Capitol Campus on January 6, 2021" 6 (Nov. 16, 2021).
[321] U.S. Dep't of Def. Inspector Gen., Transcribed Interview of William Walker (Feb. 16, 2021).
[322] Letter from Barry Loudermilk, Chairman, Comm. on H. Admin. Oversight Subcomm., to Robert Storch, Inspector Gen., Dep't of Def. (May 6, 2024) (on file with the Subcommittee).
[323] U.S. Dep't of Def. Inspector Gen., Transcribed Interview of Christopher Miller (Mar. 12, 2021), p. 12.

- Secretary McCarthy's statement that the development of a CONOP was an appropriate requirement at the height of the riot at the Capitol.

> **FINDING 5:** DoD and DoD IG knowingly and inaccurately placed blame on D.C. National Guard leadership for the delayed DoD response.

In June 2020, the DoD published an article highlighting the importance of National Guard troops in responding to civil unrest. The DoD labels the National Guard as its "First Choice" for such missions.[324] In particular, within Washington D.C., the DCNG are the DoD's designated organization to "ensure peace, order, and safety" for "federal installations and monuments."[325]

The DoD IG Report makes alarming accusations regarding the blame for the DCNG delay in responding to the U.S. Capitol on January 6, 2021. The DoD IG uses partial testimony and fails to analyze critical witness statements to construe a narrative that Major General Walker lied to Congress during a March 2021 Senate hearing, and further suggests that the DCNG is responsible for the timing of the DoD response to the Capitol on January 6, 2021.

The DoD IG Report accuses the Two-Star General and Commander of the D.C. National Guard, William Walker, of perjury.[326] On March 3, 2021, Major General Walker testified to the Senate Homeland Security and Governmental Affairs and Senate Rules and Administration Committees.[327] Major General Walker's testimony revealed information that is not favorable to Army staff and senior Pentagon officials, and thus DoD IG constructed their Report to deliberately undermine the DCNG Commander's sworn testimony.

During the hearing, Major General Walker testified that, if given approval, he could have had 150 Guardsmen to the Capitol within twenty minutes.[328] However, the DoD IG Report dismissed this claim with testimony from an unnamed witness, thereby casting doubt that the DCNG could have responded in a timely fashion on January 6:

> According to a witness, Mr. McCarthy had to reissue the deployment order to Major General Walker 30 minutes after he originally conveyed it to Major General Walker, which the witness believed contradicts Major General Walker's March 3, 2021 testimony to the Senate Homeland Security and Governmental

---

[324] David Vergun, *DOD Official: National Guard is First Choice in Response to Civil Unrest,* U.S. DEPARTMENT OF DEFENSE (June 3, 2020).

[325] David Vergun, *DOD Official: National Guard is First Choice in Response to Civil Unrest,* U.S. DEPARTMENT OF DEFENSE (June 3, 2020).

[326] Report, U.S. DEP'T OF DEF. OFF. OF INSPECTOR GEN., "Review of the DoD's Role, Responsibilities, and Actions to Prepare for and Respond to the Protest and Its Aftermath at the U.S. Capitol Campus on January 6, 2021" 6 (Nov. 16, 2021).

[327] *Examining the January 6th Attack on the U.S. Capitol: Hearing before the S. Comm. on Rules and Admin. and the S. Comm. on Homeland Sec. and Governmental Affs.,* 117th Cong., (2021).

[328] *Examining the January 6th Attack on the U.S. Capitol: Hearing before the S. Comm. on Rules and Admin. and the S. Comm. on Homeland Sec. and Governmental Affs.,* 117th Cong., (2021).

Affairs and Senate Rules and Administration Committees. The witness told us that Major General Walker's assertion to those committees that the DCNG could have responded to the Capitol in 20 minutes was not true. The witness said, "It took 27 minutes for [Major General Walker] to get the order from [Mr. McCarthy] around [4:35 PM] to actually get his wheels moving on the bus." In addition, the witness said "mischaracterization" was the word the witness would use to describe Major General Walker's response to questions from congressional committees.[329]

The DoD IG shares that the "the [unnamed] witness said 'mischaracterization' was the word the witness would use to describe Major General Walker's response to questions from congressional committees." However, the DoD IG failed to corroborate this witness's claim, suggesting that the Two-Star General was not truthful, or in any way mischaracterized hist testimony to Congress.

One other witness provided similar testimony to the DoD IG. The Subcommittee investigated these witnesses and discovered that these accusations came from two of Secretary McCarthy's junior Army staff members. The Army officers unsurprisingly attached any suggestion of delay to Major General Walker as opposed to their boss, Secretary McCarthy. The IG failed to push back on these claims or conduct any meaningful analysis. Instead, the DoD IG included these allegations as fact in their Final Report.

However, one of the aforementioned witnesses—Secretary McCarthy's junior officer—confirmed to the DoD IG that no call was placed to Major General Walker, confirming Major General Walker and his staff's consistent testimony that no call to deploy the DCNG to the Capitol was ever received prior to 5:08 PM. The DoD IG declined to include this information in its Final Report.

Secretary McCarthy's principal spokesperson and communications officer who was present with Secretary McCarthy throughout the day on January 6 provided conflicting testimony to the DoD IG.[330] The officer's testimony initially confirmed Major General Walker's position that no call was received prior to 5:08 PM. However, the DoD IG investigator provided the officer with an exhibit of the DoD's official timeline for January 6. The officer's testimony—initially consistent with Major General Walker—only shifts when she references the DoD's timeline.

> [DoD IG]: We're aware that General Walker testified to Joint Senate Committees that he didn't get word that that he was approved to move from the armory to the Capitol until a few minutes after 17:00 [5:00 PM]. What is your comment about that?

---

[329] Report, U.S. DEP'T OF DEF. OFF. OF INSPECTOR GEN., "Review of the DoD's Role, Responsibilities, and Actions to Prepare for and Respond to the Protest and Its Aftermath at the U.S. Capitol Campus on January 6, 2021" 61 (Nov. 16, 2021).

[330] U.S. Dep't of Def. Inspector Gen., Transcribed Interview of non-senior Dep't of Def. witness (Mar. 23, 2021).

[Witness]: I believe that he did get approval to the action [deploy the DCNG to the Capitol]. It's just that he [General Walker] didn't get the approval to do the specific actions until after 17:00 [5:00 PM] once everybody —once they were clear on what they were actually doing.[331]

The officer's first statement appears to confirm that DCNG Major General Walker did not get approval until 5:00 PM, only once "it was clear what they were doing" likely referring to the CONOP requirement.

The DoD IG followed up quickly during the interview as this statement from this officer did not fit the timeline suggested by other witnesses:

[DoD IG]: Are you saying that you believe that no one conveyed that level of specificity to General Walker until after 17:00 [5 PM]?

[Witness]: That's correct

[DoD IG]: And how do you know that?

[Witness]: Oh, 17:00 [5 PM]. It was after 16:00 [4 PM]. Hold on one second. It was shortly -- it was close to 17:00 [5 PM]. Yes. I mean I --

[DoD IG]: So what?

[Witness]: do not know the exact timeframe but I just know that it was close. So once a plan was developed, once everyone spoke to Acting Secretary of Defense and the Chairman that information was communicated to General Walker but I just don't know when. **On the timeline that I have**, it says 16:25 [4:25 PM].[332]

This exchange with the DoD IG investigator and officer demonstrates how quickly the officer changes their confirmation of when Major General Walker received notification to deploy to the Capitol when pressed by the interviewer; this officer merely confirms whatever timeline has been officially published. "On the timeline that I have, it says 16:25 [4:25PM]." The DoD IG does not follow up to firmly grasp or ascertain what the witness wanted to convey when revealing that Major General Walker "didn't get the approval to do the specific actions until after 17:00 [5:00 PM]."

---

[331] *Id.*
[332] *Id.* (emphasis added).

This officer declared that Major General Walker "manipulated the truth" in his testimony to the Senate Homeland Security and Governmental Affairs Committees in March of 2021:

> [Witness]: **some of the things that Major General Walker said in his testimony they were embellished** and while some of it was truthful he just wasn't telling- he wasn't telling the whole truth so **he manipulated the truth. One of the things he said was that the National Guard had all of their equipment in their trucks, in their vehicles. That's not an accurate statement. They had equipment but they only had their flack vests and helmets. They didn't have riot gear.**[333]

However, testimony from key DCNG personnel provided evidence to refute this claim.

Lieutenant Colonel Craig Hunter who was Commander of Task Force Guardian oversaw all 340 soldiers and airmen on January 6 testifies that the DCNG did in fact have riot gear in their possession:

> [Lieutenant Colonel Craig Hunter]: But on the 6th we had time that morning to put of the gear in to every individual vehicle. So every vehicle had helmets, shin guards, protective shields, vests, everything in the vehicle. So in the case the Soldiers and Airmen out there something happened they needed protection they didn't have to fall back to a different point. It [Civil Disturbance gear] was right there in their vehicles if they needed.[334]

DoD IG did not attempt to resolve this contradictory testimony based on the various witness statements.

While the actions and judgement of some DoD members on January 6 was disappointing, it was worsened by the manipulation of the DoD IG Report to cover up the actions of senior DoD staff. The Report blamed the very soldiers who were standing by, ready to come to the aid of those under attack at the Capitol. The following represents areas of concern for inaccurately blaming the D.C. National Guard for the events of January 6:

1. Blaming the DCNG for the delay. This is alarming knowing that the DCNG were ready to deploy by 3:00 PM and were intentionally held back by the Pentagon. The Subcommittee has established that the leaders in the Pentagon failed to call Major General Walker.

2. Blaming the DCNG for not being prepared for this mission, with full knowledge that countering Civil Disturbance is a core mission area, and that Secretary McCarthy personally witnessed rehearsals demonstrating this capability.

---

[333] U.S. Dep't of Def. Inspector Gen., Transcribed Interview of non-senior Dep't of Def. witness 41(Mar. 23, 2021) (emphasis added).
[334] U.S. Dep't of Def. Inspector Gen., Transcribed Interview of Lieutenant Colonel Craig Hunter (Mar. 15, 2021).

3. Blaming the DCNG Commander for "misrepresenting" his congressional testimony based on comments from junior officers. DoD IG then failed to interview any of Major General Walker's staff who were with him all day on January 6, 2021.

4. Negatively impacting the careers of several National Guard officers and enlisted Guardsmen while Pentagon general officers—whose judgement should be questioned—received promotions in both rank and command.

Fortunately, several DCNG members were willing to come forward as whistleblowers to assist in ensuring the truth comes forth.

- ### SUBCOMMITTEE WHISTLEBLOWER HEARING

April 17, 2024, Subcommittee Hearing, "Three Years Later: DC National Guard Whistleblowers Speak Out on January 6 Delay"

On April 17, 2024, the Subcommittee held a hearing with four whistleblowers who were members of the D.C. National Guard and who were heavily involved in this military unit's actions on January 6, 2021.[335] The Subcommittee was approached by approximately twenty whistleblowers, but in the interest of clarity, the Subcommittee selected the following four individuals to serve as witnesses during a Subcommittee hearing:

1. **Brigadier General Aaron Dean** – D.C. National Guard Adjutant General. As the Adjutant General, Brigadier General Dean is the second in Command at the D.C. National Guard under Major General Walker. Given the seriousness of the riots on January 6, Brigadier General Dean was involved in all significant discussions within the D.C. National Guard. He

---

[335] *Three Years Later: DC National Guard Whistleblowers Speak Out on January 6 Delay: Hearing Before the Comm. On H. Admin. Oversight Subcomm.*, 118th Cong. (2024).

was collocated with, or in constant communication with, Major General Walker all day on January 6, 2021.

2. **Colonel Earl Matthews** – D.C. National Guard Staff Judge Advocate. Given the seriousness of the riots on January 6, Colonel Matthews was involved in all senior-level DCNG discussions and decisions on that day.

3. **Captain Timothy Nick** – Aide-de-Camp to Major General William Walker. As the Aide to Major General Walker, Captain Nick's responsibilities included being with the Commander and documenting all critical events that happened on this hectic day.

4. **Command Sergeant Major Michael Brooks** – Command Sergeant Major and Senior Enlisted Advisor. While there are many officers in the chain of command, no senior leader has a significant discussion or makes an impactful decision without the involvement and concurrence of their senior enlisted advisor. Command Sergeant Major Brooks is responsible for the more than 2,000 enlisted personnel that make up the D.C. National Guard.

CHRISTOPHER MILLER
ACTING SECRETARY OF DEFENSE

RYAN MCCARTHY
SECRETARY OF THE ARMY

LTG WALTER PIATT
DIRECTOR OF ARMY STAFF

GEN CHARLES FLYNN
DEPUTY CHIEF OF STAFF
FOR ARMY OPERATIONS,
PLANS, AND TRAINING

MG WILLIAM WALKER
COMMANDING GENERAL,
DC NATIONAL GUARD

COL EARL MATTHEWS
JUDGE ADVOCATE, U.S. ARMY

CSM MICHAEL BROOKS
SENIOR ENLISTED OFFICER

BG AARON DEAN
ADJUTANT GENERAL

CPT TIMOTHY NICK
AIDE-DE-CAMP TO
MG WALKER

Many current and former members of the DCNG approached the Subcommittee with concerns about the DoD IG Report. The Subcommittee conducted transcribed interviews and selected these four DCNG personnel who were closest to the operations, decision-making and communications of the DCNG on January 6, 2021.[336]

All four whistleblowers who appeared as witnesses at the April 17, 2024, Subcommittee hearing reported directly to the Commanding General of the DCNG William Walker on January 6, 2021. All four whistleblowers testified under oath that claims made in the DoD IG Report are wholly inaccurate, specifically regarding alleged phone calls between Secretary of the Army Ryan McCarthy and Major General William Walker at 3:05 PM and 4:35 PM on January 6, 2021.[337] All four whistleblowers maintain consistent accounts of the events on January 6, 2021: the D.C. National Guard were not given approval to deploy to the US Capitol by the Pentagon chain of command until after 5pm on January 6, 2021.[338] Not a single D.C. National Guardsman who testified to the Subcommittee on April 17, 2024, was interviewed by the DoD IG to construct the DoD IG Report[339].

On March 6, 2024, Colonel Matthews participated in a bipartisan transcribed interview with the Subcommittee.[340] Colonel Matthews testified about the condition of the soldiers at the D.C. Armory as they waited several hours for the deployment order from the Pentagon to respond to the violence at the U.S. Capitol.

> "[Colonel Matthews]: And we have people at the D.C. Armory who are able to help, and they're not moving. And they're not allowed to move. They're not allowed to go down there."[341]

On March 14, 2024, Command Sergeant Major Brooks participated in a transcribed interview with the Subcommittee.[342] Command Sergeant Major Brooks shared candid details regarding the DCNG delay on January 6.

[336] Comm. On H. Admin. Oversight Subcomm., Transcribed Interview of Colonel Earl Matthews (Mar. 6, 2024); Comm. On H. Admin. Oversight Subcomm., Transcribed Interview of Command Sergeant Major Michael Brooks (Mar. 14, 2024); Comm. On H. Admin. Oversight Subcomm., Transcribed Interview of Brigadier General Aaron Dean (Mar. 26, 2024); Comm. On H. Admin. Oversight Subcomm., Transcribed Interview of Captain Timothy Nick (Apr. 9, 2024).
[337] *Three Years Later: DC National Guard Whistleblowers Speak Out on January 6 Delay: Hearing Before the Comm. On H. Admin. Oversight Subcomm.,* 118th Cong. (2024).
[338] *Id.*
[339] U.S. DEP'T OF DEF. INSPECTOR GEN., Report Witness List (on file with the Subcommittee).
[340] Comm. on H. Admin. Oversight Subcomm., Transcribed Interview of Earl Matthews (Mar. 6, 2024).
[341] *Id.* at 57.
[342] Comm. On H. Admin. Oversight Subcomm., Transcribed Interview of Michael Brooks (Mar. 14, 2024).

"[Command Sergeant Major Brooks]: Like, literally sitting on a bus, just waiting to drive to the Capitol and do the best they could to support the Capitol Police."[343]

On March 26, 2024, Brigadier General Aaron Dean participated in a transcribed interview with the Subcommittee.[344] Brigadier General Dean confirmed that the DCNG did not receive any orders to deploy to the Capitol until after 5:00 PM on January 6, 2021.

> "[Brigadier General Aaron Dean]: There were no phone calls made. There was no one telling anybody to move toward the Capitol prior to 5 o'clock."[345]

Brigadier General Aaron Dean also detailed the concern about 'optics' from senior Army staff at the Pentagon in his interview with the Subcommittee:

> "[Brigadier General Aaron Dean]: there was a bunch of conversation within that initial call [2:30 PM conference call]. And then General Piatt was the one that said, 'I am concerned about optics of Guardsmen being at the Capitol.' And I thought to myself, 'Okay. I'm not sure why we're concerned about optics when it comes to, you know, saving lives and preventing loss of property, but okay.'"[346]

On April 9, 2024, Captain Timothy Nick participated in a transcribed interview with the Subcommittee.[347] Major General Walker's Aide-de-Camp testified that DCNG were struggling to receive any orders whatsoever from Pentagon leadership:

> "[Captain Nick]: I can't speak to what the Pentagon was doing. I don't know why it took almost 3 hours to make a decision, whether it was a crisis of leadership at the time or decision paralysis at the Pentagon from key senior leaders. It was definitely delayed.

> And some of the things that the General's staff were asking for, in my eyes, were not relevant for the situation, concept of operations. It seemed like they wanted a PowerPoint presentation with symbols and signs of where we're going. Under the circumstances that's not feasible."[348]

The sworn testimony from the interviews and the subsequent Subcommittee hearing on April 17, 2024, from these four District of Columbia National Guardsmen, contradicts evidence and claims suggested by the conclusions in the November 2021 DoD IG Report. The Subcommittee does not have a vested interest in supporting either the claims or narratives of the whistleblowers against the DoD IG Report. As an oversight entity, the Subcommittee is simply highlighting the lack of independent and rigorous analysis by the DoD IG in their failure to interview the D.C.

---

[343] *Id.* at 64.

[344] Comm. On H. Admin. Oversight Subcomm., Transcribed Interview of Aaron Dean (Mar. 26, 2024).

[345] *Id.* at 19.

[346] *Id.* at 26.

[347] Comm. On H. Admin. Oversight Subcomm., Transcribed Interview of Timothy Nick (Apr. 9, 2024).

[348] *Id.* at 64-65.

National Guard witnesses who have maintained a different account of DoD events on January 6, 2021.

> **FINDING 6:** DoD IG was not responsive to the Subcommittee's requests, and, at times, obstructed the Subcommittee's work. The Subcommittee has detected an inappropriately close relationship between the DoD Inspector General and DoD which compromises the Inspector General's ability to conduct objective oversight.

It is the Subcommittee's assessment of the DoD IG's investigation of the events on January 6, 2021, that the DoD IG is inappropriately deferential to the DoD. As such, the DoD IG may be incapable of providing an unbiased, independent review of DoD actions. The following points outline the interactions of the Subcommittee and DoD IG that illustrate this finding. Additionally, our interactions with the governing body overseeing the DoD IG, the Council of the Inspectors General on Integrity and Efficiency ("CIGIE"), further raise concerns about the ability for IG's to remain unbiased from the agencies and departments tasked with overseeing.

Subcommittee Interactions with the Department of Defense Inspector General

On February 29, 2024, Chairman Loudermilk submitted a letter to DoD Inspector General Robert Storch requesting an unredacted version of Report No. DODIG-2022-039, as well as witness transcripts used to construct the report.[349] In conducting its oversight responsibilities, the Subcommittee requested these materials to examine the evidence used to support the DoD IG Report's conclusion. Chairman Loudermilk explicitly asks DoD Inspector General Storch:

"As part of my investigation into the security failures that occurred on January 6, 2021, it is crucial for the Subcommittee to review records and materials your office holds regarding that day."

Nearly five weeks later, on April 2, 2024, the DoD IG replied stating that it could not support Chairman Loudermilk's request for an unredacted version of Report No. DODIG-2022-039 as well as witness interview transcripts. Inspector General Storch failed to provide the materials requested by Chairman Loudermilk on February 29, 2024. According to the DoD IG, the information which the Subcommittee requested was "inappropriate" and "could not be released outside the Executive Branch" under direction of the Department of the Army and the Federal Bureau of Investigation ("FBI"):[350]

---

[349] Letter from Barry Loudermilk, Chairman, Comm. on H. Admin. Oversight Subcomm., to Robert Storch, Inspector Gen., Dep't of Def. (Feb. 29, 2024) (on file with the Subcommittee).
[350] Letter from Robert Storch, Inspector Gen., Dep't of Def., to Barry Loudermilk, Chairman, Comm. on H. Admin. Oversight Subcomm. (Apr. 2, 2024) (on file with the Subcommittee).

"This information, determined by the Army and FBI to be controlled unclassified information that could not be released outside the Executive Branch, is not within my office's authority to release."[351]

In their April 2, 2024, response, the DoD IG denied the Subcommittee's request for an unredacted version of Report 2022-039 and witness transcripts. Inspector General Storch asserted that the requested information "contains information not within unilateral authority of the DoD OIG to release."[352]

After months of bureaucratic stonewalling and continued negotiations, on June 13, 2024, the DoD IG agreed for the Subcommittee to conduct an in camera review of minimally redacted witness transcripts used to construct the DoD IG Report and a minimally redacted version of the DoD IG Report. Strangely, Office of the Secretary of Defense ("OSD") personnel were copied on email chains between the Subcommittee and DoD IG and interfered with Subcommittee's ability to work in good faith with the DoD IG.

The Subcommittee participated in the in camera review of DoD IG documents at the Pentagon on June 20 and 21, 2024. However, days before the in camera review, the Office of the Secretary of Defense restricted the Subcommittee personnel who could attend the review and denied access to the Pentagon for certain Subcommittee part-time staff.

Unfortunately, the Subcommittee's in camera visit to the Pentagon confirmed suspicions that the DoD IG failed to conduct a thorough investigation. The Inspector General staff present at the *in-camera* could not answer basic questions pertaining to witness statements in transcribed interviews and had to contact investigators for clarification. Furthermore, the IG withheld a certain witness interview transcript, which only became apparent when Subcommittee staff noticed that the first copy of the transcript concluded with the DoD IG suggesting they would conduct another interview in the future (DoD IG did not produce the missing transcript until the second day of the in camera review).

It became clear to Chairman Loudermilk that the good faith negotiation that led to an in camera review was not sufficient for the Subcommittee to effectively perform its oversight duties pertaining to the safety of the U.S. Capitol.[353] Following further negotiations, on July 2, 2024, the DoD Office of General Counsel coordinating with the DoD IG agreed to provide the Subcommittee with "lightly redacted" versions of witness transcripts by July 14, 2024.[354] The DoD IG failed to meet the July 14, 2024, deadline and explained that the delay was due to

---

[351] *Id.*
[352] *Id.*
[353] Email from Staff, Comm. on H. Admin. Oversight Subcomm., to Dave Core, Principal Deputy Gen. Couns., Off. of the Inspector Gen. of the Dep't of Defense, and Ed Richards, Senior Assistant Deputy Gen. Couns., Off. of the Sec'y of Defense (July 1, 2024) (on file with the Subcommittee).
[354] Email from Ed Richards, Senior Assistant Deputy Gen. Couns., Off. of the Sec'y of Defense, to Staff, Comm. on H. Admin. Oversight Subcomm. (July 2, 2024) (on file with the Subcommittee).

"interagency equities", which, to this day, the Subcommittee does not understand. Finally, on August 21, 2024, all forty-three DoD IG witness transcripts were given to the Subcommittee.

On September 5, 2024, the Subcommittee released all, previously concealed for years by the DoD, witness interviews transcripts to the public. The witness testimonies in these, now publicly released, interviews contain evidence for two new revelations: senior Pentagon officials dismissed President Trump's directives to ensure safety for the demonstrations on January 6, 2021, and intentionally delayed deployment of the D.C. National Guard due to concerns over 'optics' [see **Finding 1** and **Finding 2** in this document].

It is extremely concerning and inappropriate for the exact entity which the Inspector General is tasked with overseeing obstructs or influences the investigative process and communications. The DoD IG is supposed to be an impartial and independent watchdog; however, it is clear to the Subcommittee that the Office of the Secretary of Defense–based on our interactions throughout the in camera review process–is intimately involved in the operations of the DoD IG. The Subcommittee's suspicions of a flawed DoD IG Report were confirmed due to the DoD's lack of transparency with the Subcommittee's investigation, contrived bureaucratic obstacles, and the DoD initially concealing information requested by appropriate congressional oversight authority.

It appears that DODIG-2022-039's primary purpose was to construct a narrative suited to the DoD's interests. A story that portrayed DoD in a favorable light and ensured that no DoD personnel, particularly high-ranking officials, broke the law. This is not the purpose of any Inspector General.

The Subcommittee recommends that a review is conducted to see if this behavior is unique to this report or, as we suspect, that this incestuous behavior is common among the DoD IG office.

Subcommittee Interactions with the Council of the Inspector's General on Integrity and Efficiency:

On July 23, 2024, the Chair of the Council of the Inspectors General on Integrity and Efficiency ("CIGIE"), Hon. Mark Greenblatt testified before the House Committee on Oversight and Accountability, Subcommittee on Government Operations and the Federal Workforce.[355]

At this hearing Subcommittee Chairman Loudermilk waived-on to ask the CIGIE Chairman whether factually inaccurate reports, such as DoD IG 2022-039, can be amended or revised. Indeed, Mr. Greenblatt asserted that this is possible. Therefore, the Subcommittee submitted the following Questions for the Record to CIGIE:

---

[355] *Oversight of the Council of the Inspectors General on Integrity and Efficiency: Hearing before the S. Comm. on Gov't Operations and the Fed. Workforce.*, 118th Cong. (2024) (testimony Mark L. Greenblatt, Chairman, Council of the Inspector General on Integrity and Efficiency).

- Does CIGIE provide guidance for IGs on how to retract or revise reports that are found to contain errors? If so, please provide that guidance. If not, please explain why.

- In your testimony on July 23, when asked about the process to retract or correct an IG report, you stated: "I've seen that happen in the past, sir. And we try to get it right – get the right answer, and if we get it wrong, I think it would be wholly appropriate to take down whatever is wrong and replace it with something that is factually accurate."

  - What steps do we, as an Oversight Subcommittee, take to begin the process of correcting the errors in DoD IG Report No. DODIG-2022-039?

  - In this case, are corrections made to the existing report, an addendum to the existing report, or is a new report produced?

  - What is CIGIE's role in the evaluation of whether an IG report that contains errors must be corrected?

In addition, the Subcommittee is working to achieve greater clarity as to why a "Review" was selected as the method selected to consider the DoD's roles, responsibilities and actions on January 6.

According to the DoD IG website, the various components of the organization can include audits, investigations, and evaluations.[356] However, a "Review" was pursued by the DOD IG. Specifically, the scope of investigation is detailed on the first page of DoD IG 2022-039: "We evaluated whether the DoD's actions were appropriate and supported by requirements. We also examined whether the DoD complied with applicable laws, regulations, and other guidance in its response to requests for assistance." As is elucidated by the piecemeal logic and inconsistent testimony to construct the narrative in the report, the document fails to analyze or question the actions and decisions of senior DoD officials. In other words, the DoD IG conducted a storytelling operation without questioning whether each witnesses' story led to a successful outcome regarding DoD's reaction to the events of the Capitol on January 6.

To that end, the Subcommittee included the following in Question for the Record to CIGIE:

- DODIG-2022-039 could have been executed as an Evaluation, Administrative Investigation or an Audit, according to the Organization guidance on the DoD IG website, however it was selected to be conducted as a "Review".

  - Please explain the difference between a "Review" from other types of reports.

---

[356] DEP'T OF DEFENSE OFF. OF INSPECTOR GEN., *About us* (accessed Nov. 14, 2024).

- o Does CIGIE have any insight as to why DoD IG selected a "Review" for this investigation?

- o DODIG-2022-039 attempted to identify the DoD's actions on January 6, however failed to conduct any analysis to the impact of these actions to the DoD's response to the events on January 6. Is a "Review" prohibited from conducting analysis on crucial actions that DoD chose to pursue?

- o Does CIGIE believe that DODIG-2022-0039 should have been a "Review" or would an Administrative Investigation have been a better option for this case?

Prior to the July 2024 hearing with Chairman Greenblatt, the Subcommittee had reached out to CIGIE over concerns with the DoD IG Report. Unfortunately, CIGIE did not respond to the Subcommittee's query, and instead directly forwarded our questions to the DoD IG. As of the date of publication, the Subcommittee has yet to receive any responses from CIGIE. Therefore, the Subcommittee lacks confidence in CIGIE's ability to successfully play its role as the oversight entity for Inspectors General.

Finally, the Subcommittee must note that our relationship with DoD IG and CIGIE is only representative of a singular query with these organizations and thus may not represent systemic issues. The Subcommittee is only concerned with a singular flawed Report and has only discovered this troubling lack of oversight and professionalism from both the DoD IG and CIGIE throughout our investigation. The Subcommittee acknowledges that a singular sample size is not sufficient to conclude that our concerns are present throughout the entirety of both organizations. Nonetheless, our finding that the DoD IG and DoD have collaborated to impede the Subcommittee's investigation and furthermore that the Inspectors General watchdog is not holding the DoD IG accountable remains troubling in our estimation.

Letters
- 2/29/24 Letter from Barry Loudermilk to Robert Storch
  - o Record Production Request
- 5/6/24 Letter from Barry Loudermilk to Robert Storch
  - o Unredacted Record Production Request
- 5/16/24 Letter from Barry Loudermilk to Secretary Austin
  - o DOD IG Production Authorization
- 5/23/24 Letter from Barry Loudermilk to David Zaslav
  - o Documentary Footage Request
- 5/28/24 Letter from Barry Loudermilk to Lloyd Austin
  - o Unredacted Record Production Request
- 6/17/24 Letter from Barry Loudermilk to David Zaslav
  - o Record Preservation Request
- 6/25/24 Letter from Barry Loudermilk to David Zaslav

- o Documentary Footage Request
- 8/28/24 Letter from Barry Loudermilk to William McFarland
  - o National Guard Record Production Request
- 11/21/24 Letter from Barry Loudermilk to Robert Storch
  - o Correct the Flawed DoD IG Report Request

Due to the broad response and reaction to January 6, 2021, from across the federal government, many agency watchdogs opened independent investigations into their respective agency or department's role in planning for and responding to January 6. These independent watchdogs, also known as Inspectors General ("IG") were statutorily created to report directly to Congress about the activities and practices of the agency they are assigned.[357] IGs are also tasked with detecting and preventing waste, fraud, and abuse throughout the government.[358]

The Subcommittee relied heavily on IGs for their independent, fact-based analysis of the actions of their individual department or agency. However, there has been a concerning trend among IGs where their independence to conduct their work is strained by the agency they are tasked to oversee. For example, in the Subcommittee's work with the Department of Homeland Security ("DHS") IG, we uncovered that DHS threatened to withhold access to the IG if they published a report that was not cleared by DHS. After DHS accepted our request for an in camera review of its unredacted IG report, it is the Subcommittee's opinion that significant redactions DHS imposed served only to obscure culpability or failures. The Subcommittee maintains that IGs are independent entities, and it is not acceptable for an agency to threaten to withhold access to an IG.

On July 23, 2024, Chairman Loudermilk waived on to a Committee on Oversight and Accountability, Subcommittee on Government Operations and the Federal Workforce hearing with the Chair of the Council of the Inspectors General on Integrity and Efficiency ("CIGIE"), Mark Greenblatt. CIGIE is tasked with overseeing IGs and setting standards for IG audits, inspections, evaluations, and investigations.[359] During this hearing, Chair Greenblatt indicated that it would never be acceptable for an agency to condition access based on the favorability of reports.[360]

After this hearing, Chairman Loudermilk submitted over fifty Questions for the Record ("QFRs") to Chair Greenblatt seeking answers about IG operations, independence issues, and process issues at CIGIE. To date, the Subcommittee, nor the Committee on Oversight and Accountability, have received answers to these QFRs. In response to these developments, Chairman Loudermilk sent a letter to DHS Secretary Mayorkas on July 24, 2024, expressing concern that two of the three reports about DHS' actions on January 6 had not yet been released.[361] Chairman Loudermilk indicated in this letter that the Subcommittee was aware that

---

[357] CONGRESSIONAL RESEARCH SERVICE, CRS Report R45450, STATUTORY INSPECTORS GENERAL IN THE FEDERAL GOVERNMENT: A PRIMER (2023).
[358] Id.
[359] COUNCIL OF THE INSPECTORS GENERAL ON INTEGRITY AND EFFICIENCY, Mission (Accessed Dec. 2, 2024).
[360] Committee on House Administration, Oversight Subcommittee Chairman Loudermilk Questions CIGIE Chairman Greenblatt, YOUTUBE (July 23, 2024).
[361] Letter from Barry Loudermilk, Chairman, Comm. on H. Admin. Oversight Subcomm., to Alejandro Mayorkas, Secretary, Dep't of Homeland Security (July 24, 2024) (on file with the Subcommittee).

one of these reports was finalized and had been waiting for DHS approval since April 2024—well past the standard thirty days given to departments to review IG reports.[362] DHS responded on August 1, 2024, stating that the Subcommittee's concerns were invalid because the report was released that day.[363] Without Chairman Loudermilk's persistent inquiries, DHS would have likely delayed the release of this report indefinitely.

Additionally, Chairman Loudermilk and Senator Chuck Grassley sent a letter to DHS Secretary Mayorkas on August 20, 2024, outlining their concerns of access issues for the DHS IG, citing the Semiannual Reports spanning back to September 2021.[364] The Subcommittee did not receive a response from DHS, and was told by the Department that while these allegations have previously been addressed in their entirety by DHS, the timeline envisioned in the letter was "not feasible." DHS was asked to respond by August 27, 2024.[365]

On August 20, 2024, Chairman Loudermilk and Senator Grassley also sent a letter to the DHS IG requesting certain documents—that the Subcommittee had already seen but were not turned over by the DHS IG—to back up the IG's continued claims of access issues and tampering by DHS.[366] The DHS IG is refusing to cooperate further with the Subcommittee on this issue.

The Subcommittee is committed to working with the committees of jurisdiction to provide meaningful reforms that protect the integrity and independence of IGs and allow these crucial watchdogs to operate independently of their department or agency without fear of retribution, hindering future investigations.

Letters
- 2/8/24 Letter from Barry Loudermilk to Joseph Cuffari
  - Unredacted Report Production Request
- 4/23/24 Letter from Barry Loudermilk to Joseph Cuffari
  - Report Redaction Adjustment Request
- 5/9/24 Letter from Barry Loudermilk to Secretary Mayorkas
  - Report Redaction Adjustment Request
- 7/24/24 Letter from Barry Loudermilk to Secretary Mayorkas
  - Outstanding Reports Inquiry

---

[362] *Id.*

[363] Letter from Zephranie Buetow, Assistant Sec'y for Legis. Affs., to Barry Loudermilk, Chairman, Comm. on H. Admin. Oversight Subcomm., (Aug. 1, 2024) (on file with the Subcommittee).

[364] Letter from Chuck Grassley, Senator, and Barry Loudermilk, Chairman, Comm. on H. Admin. Oversight Subcomm., to Alejandro Mayorkas, Secretary, Dep't of Homeland Security (Aug. 20, 2024) (on file with the Subcommittee).

[365] Email from Dep't of Homeland Affs Off. of Legis. Affs., to Staff, Comm. on H. Admin. Oversight Subcomm. (Sept. 25, 2024) (on file with the Subcommittee).

[366] Letter from Chuck Grassley, Senator, and Barry Loudermilk, Chairman, Comm. on H. Admin. Oversight Subcomm., to Alejandro Mayorkas, Secretary, Dep't of Homeland Security (Aug. 20, 2024) (on file with the Subcommittee).

- 7/25/24 Letter from Barry Loudermilk to Ronald Rowe
  - Communications with Inspector General Inquiry
- 8/20/24 Letter from Barry Loudermilk and Senator Grassley to Joseph Cuffari
  - Report Production Request
- 8/20/24 Letter from Barry Loudermilk and Senator Grassley to Secretary Mayorkas
  - DHS Obstruction Inquiry into DHS OIG

The United States Capitol Police maintains a network of nearly 1,600 closed circuit television ("CCTV") cameras within and around the United States Capitol as part of their mission to protect the U.S. Capitol, Members of Congress, and the public.

When the Subcommittee received USCP CCTV footage from the U.S. Capitol on January 5 and 6, 2021, Chairman Loudermilk committed to releasing as much footage as security considerations would allow. Over more than six months, the Subcommittee made more than 44,000 hours of CCTV footage publicly available on Rumble. These periodic releases enabled the American people to freely view all the events of January 5 and 6 in and around the U.S. Capitol, seeing the truth of the events from that day for themselves.

Additionally, since November 20, 2023, the Subcommittee has maintained a viewing room for all CCTV footage from the U.S. Capitol. This viewing room enabled media organizations, criminal defendants, and U.S. citizens the ability to review each minute of the USCP CCTV footage in person.

As a result of the Subcommittee's terminal room and video releases, there have been significant advances into our investigation of the events of January 6, 2021. This includes investigative developments into the gallows constructed on U.S. Capitol grounds, as well as leads in the pipe bombs placed at the Democratic National Committee ("DNC") and Republican National Committee ("RNC"). The Subcommittee's review and release of video footage has enabled greater transparency and review of the law enforcement and Department of Defense responses to the Capitol on January 6.

The Subcommittee's substantial investigation into the pipe bomb will be released as its own standalone report in conjunction with the House Committee on the Judiciary. The Committees' joint report examines **1) the law enforcement response to the pipe bombs** and **2) the investigation into the pipe bomb suspect.** The goal of the Committees' investigation was to conduct a thorough review of the security failures related to the pipe bombs' discovery and provide transparency–nearly four years later–on the investigation into the individual who planted the devices.

Letters

- 6/9/23 Letter from Barry Loudermilk to Thomas Manger January 6, 2024 CCTV Footage Request

Some of the most enduring and sensationalized images from the events of January 6, 2021, revolve around the construction of a makeshift gallows next to the reflecting on the west side of the United States Capitol.[367] The symbology of the gallows was adopted by most major newspapers, and the Select Committee featured used photograph of the gallows as the backdrop for several of its hearings.[368] Despite the notoriety of the gallows, to date, none of the individuals involved in constructing the structure have been publicly identified by law enforcement. Speaker Pelosi's partisan Select Committee did not include any investigation into the gallows or its creators in its Final Report, and it is unclear whether Select Committee investigated its favorite set piece at all. In contrast, Chairman Loudermilk and the Subcommittee have conducted a thorough investigation of the gallows, including communicating directly with multiple federal agencies and the Architect of the Capitol, and performed a frame-by-frame review of countless hours of surveillance footage.

Through the Subcommittee's review of United States Capitol Police ("USCP") closed circuit television ("CCTV") footage, a group of five individuals are first spotted at 6:25 AM on January 6, 2021, wheeling a large amount of lumber through the western crosswalk at First Street NW and C Street NW, moving south towards Union Square.[369]

---

[367] Scott MacFarlane, *Newly obtained video shows movement of group suspected of constructing Jan. 6 gallows hours before Capitol siege*, CBS NEWS (Mar. 18, 2024).

[368] *On the Jan. 6th Investigation: Hearing before the H. Select Comm. to Investigate the Jan. 6th Attack on the United States Capitol,* 117th Cong (2022).

[369] Videotape: Camera 07212 – Jan. 6, at 6:25 AM (U.S. Capitol Police) (on file with the Subcommittee).

The group continues south on First Street and Louisiana Avenue.[370] They then cross Constitution Avenue and enter Capitol property at Union Square at 6:31 AM.[371]

For the next fifty-five minutes, the group assembled the structure. Through a review of images and artifacts collected by the National Museum of American obtained by the Subcommittee, it is clear that the group had planned to build this particular construction in advance.[372] The lumber used in the construction had corresponding numbers written on them in black marker that facilitated a rapid construction of the gallows' base. The group did not attach the cross bar at the top of the gallows at this time.

The footage shows an apparent group leader, identifiable by a long trench coat, white scarf, fedora-style hat, and carrying a cane. During the fifty-five-minute construction, the apparent leader and one other individual temporarily depart the site of the gallows.[373] They were seen walking north on 3rd Street NW before disappearing from view behind the United States Department of Labor's ("DOL") building on the corner of 3rd Street NW and Constitution Avenue NW.[374]

---

[370] Videotape: Camera 3189 – Jan. 6, at 6:28 AM (U.S. Capitol Police) (on file with the Subcommittee).
[371] Videotape: Camera 3183 – Jan. 6, at 6:31 AM (U.S. Capitol Police) (on file with the Subcommittee).
[372] Email from Frank Blazich, Curator, Nat'l Museum Am. Hist. to Tyler Hoover, Prof. Staff Member, Comm. on H. Admin. Oversight Subcomm. (Sept. 4, 2024) (on file with the Subcommittee).
[373] Videotape: Camera 3183 – Jan. 6, at 6:47 AM (U.S. Capitol Police) (on file with the Subcommittee).
[374] Videotape: Camera 0514 – Jan. 6, at 6:48 AM (U.S. Capitol Police) (on file with the Subcommittee).

The two men emerge at the intersection of 3rd Street NW and Constitution Avenue NW twenty minutes later with coffee. They proceed to rejoin the group and help finish assembling the gallows.[375] At 7:18 AM, the entire group departs Union Square,[376] again crossing the same intersection heading north, and disappear from view behind the DOL building.[377]

[375] Videotape: Camera 0514 – Jan. 6, at 7:09 AM (U.S. Capitol Police) (on file with the Subcommittee).
[376] Videotape: Camera 3183 – Jan. 6, at 7:18 AM (U.S. Capitol Police) (on file with the Subcommittee).
[377] Videotape: Camera 0514 – Jan. 6, at 7:20 AM (U.S. Capitol Police) (on file with the Subcommittee).

The group then returned to the site of the partial gallows at approximately 1:00 PM, at which point they attached the structure's crossbeam and a noose made of bright orange rope.[378]

The Subcommittee's review of USCP CCTV footage was useful to identify the timing and route taken by the group, but not sufficient to identify the individuals involved in the gallows. Unfortunately, the USCP CCTV cameras that captured the group were too distant to allow for effective facial identification.

The Subcommittee identified at least four buildings located along the group's route that would have likely recorded footage with greater image fidelity. These include the headquarters of the Federal Bureau of Prisons, the U.S. Department of Labor's Frances Perkins Building, the U.S. District Court building for the District of Columbia, and a prominent law firm.

The following map illustrates the path taken by the group to the gallows' construction site, and the locations of the buildings that likely recorded their activity.

---

[378] Press Release, COMM. ON H. ADMIN. OVERSIGHT SUBCOMM., Barry Loudermilk Releases New Information in the January 6, 2021 Gallows Investigation (Feb. 23, 2024).

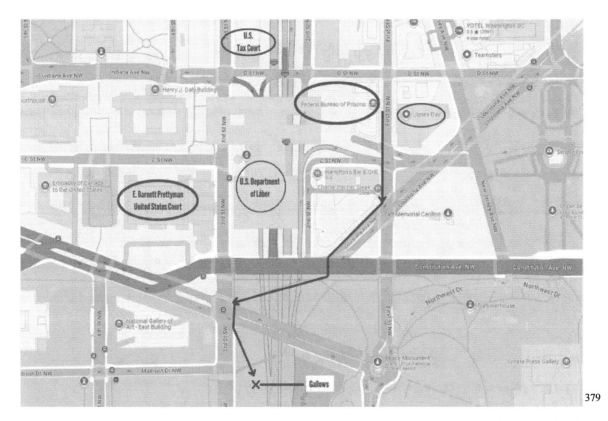

379

The Subcommittee's review of commercially available street-view photographs taken in the months prior to January 6, 2021, reveal that each of the buildings had external cameras that would have likely captured the group of gallows constructors with much more clarity than that available from USCP CCTV.

The following map shows that in the case of the DOL and D.C. District Court buildings, the cameras would have likely captured two of the constructors at least three times on January 6.

---

379 Google LLC, *Google Maps* (2024) (screenshot of the location of the route taken by the gallows constructors to the construction site on Capitol grounds).

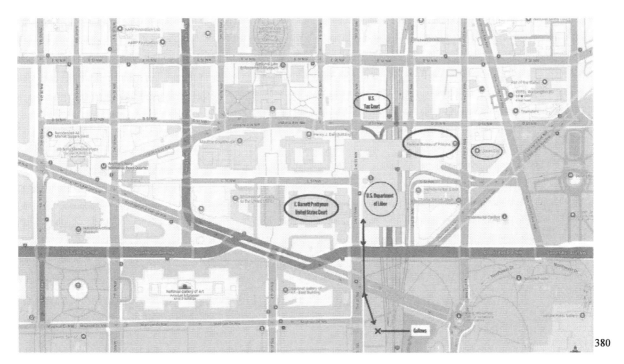

380

The Subcommittee contacted the DOL,[381] D.C. District Court,[382] U.S. Tax Court,[383] Federal Bureau of Prisons,[384] and the law firm's building manager[385] to ask if they were ever contacted by any federal agency or congressional committee to provide video footage for January 6, 2021. Shockingly, each entity confirmed that they were never contacted for this footage by any government entity, including the FBI and the Select Committee.

Both the Select Committee and the FBI had access to the same USCP CCTV footage available to the Subcommittee, yet neither entity made any effort to obtain additional, clear video that could have led to the identification of the individuals in question. It is unclear what the Select Committee or FBI did to investigate the gallows, if anything, but the Subcommittee was able to identify previously unreleased information, including the route taken by the gallows constructors on January 6, 2021.

[380] Google LLC, *Google Maps* (2024) (screenshot of the location of the route taken by the gallows constructors to the construction site on Capitol grounds).

[381] Letter from the U.S. Dep't of Lab., to Barry Loudermilk, Chairman, Comm. on H. Admin. Oversight Subcomm. (May 15, 2024) (on file with the Subcommittee).

[382] Email from D.C. Dist. Ct. to Barry Loudermilk, Chairman, Comm. on H. Admin. Oversight Subcomm. (Oct. 10, 2024) (on file with the Subcommittee).

[383] Email from the U.S. T.C. to Barry Loudermilk, Chairman, Comm. on H. Admin. Oversight Subcomm. (May 17, 2024) (on file with the Subcommittee).

[384] Email from the Fed. Bureau of Prisons Off. of Legis. Affs. to Barry Loudermilk, Chairman, Comm. on H. Admin. Oversight Subcomm. (December 5, 2024) (on file with the Subcommittee).

[385] Email from Jamestown Urban Mgmt. to Barry Loudermilk, Chairman, Comm. on H. Admin. Oversight Subcomm. (Sept. 19, 2024) (on file with the Subcommittee).

United States Capitol Police guidelines prohibit the construction of temporary structures on Capitol grounds.[386] Despite this, USCP made no effort to prevent the construction of the gallows, and the USCP CCTV footage confirms that the gallows remained on Capitol grounds for a full twenty-six hours with no effort to have them removed.[387] Multiple USCP cameras face the location of the gallows on the west side of the Capitol, and several USCP officers were within the vicinity of the gallows, yet no officers ever approached the constructors during the fifty-five minutes spent building the gallows on Capitol property, no radio calls or notifications were distributed to officers about the presence of an illegal structure on Capitol grounds, and no officers responded to the structure at any time.[388]

The gallows were finally removed at roughly 9:06 AM on January 7, 2021,[389] after USCP ignored the structure overnight. USCP radio transmissions appear to indicate that there was no order or request to investigate the gallows, and USCP video footage reveals that no law enforcement entity investigated the structure before it was removed and destroyed. Instead, USCP video footage shows Architect of the Capitol ("AOC") employees loading the structure into the back of a dump truck and crushing it using a forklift. The AOC then discarded the now-broken lumber alongside the other refuse left on Capitol Grounds from January 6. See a more detailed analysis in Appendix Two.

Internal emails among USCP leadership indicate a lack of knowledge as to the location of the gallows remnants.[390] These emails confirm the Subcommittee's findings. When questioned by the Subcommittee, AOC responded that they had no conversations with the FBI, USCP, or any other entity about the gallows on or after January 6, and that the remnants of the gallows were "transported to a waste management facility for disposal" alongside other trash and debris.[391] In fact, the only known surviving portion of the gallows structure is the noose, which was recovered by a Dutch journalist and given to the FBI.[392]

The Subcommittee identified shocking failures by the FBI, USCP, AOC, the Select Committee, and other federal agencies. These include:

---

[386] UNITED STATES CAPITOL POLICE, GUIDELINES FOR CONDUCTING AN EVENT ON UNITED STATES CAPITOL GROUNDS (updated Jan. 2024).

[387] Scott MacFarlane, *Newly obtained video shows movement of group suspected of constructing Jan. 6 gallows hours before Capitol siege*, CBS NEWS (Mar. 18, 2024).

[388] Letter from the U.S. Capitol Police to Barry Loudermilk, Chairman, Comm. on H. Admin. Oversight Subcomm. (Aug. 12, 2024) (on file with the Subcommittee).

[389] Videotape: Camera 0908 – Jan. 7, at 9:06 AM (U.S. Capitol Police) (on file with the Subcommittee).

[390] Email Thomas DiBiase, Gen. Couns., U.S. Capitol Police, to Timothy Barber, Pub. Info. Off., U.S. Capitol Police (Sept. 13, 2021) (on file with the Subcommittee).

[391] Letter from the Architect of the Capitol to Barry Loudermilk, Chairman, Comm. on H. Admin. Oversight Subcomm. (Oct. 28, 2024) (on file with the Subcommittee).

[392] Scott MacFarlane, *Noose displayed at Capitol insurrection in FBI's custody*, NBC WASHINGTON (November 1, 2021).

1. The failure to discover or prevent the construction of gallows on United States Capitol property;

2. The failure to respond to the presence of gallows on Capitol property for approximately twenty-six hours, including nearly five hours before crowds began to arrive at the Capitol from the Ellipse, and the roughly fifteen hours between the removal of protestors from Capitol property and the dismantling of the gallows;

3. The failure to preserve or retain the gallows, a key component of the events and imagery of January 6, and instead destroying and disposing of the structure; and

4. The failure to investigate the creation of the gallows, make any effort to track the route of its constructors, or determine their identity by reviewing critical footage available from partner federal agencies.

Through these failures, vital physical and visual evidence has been destroyed or deleted that would have greatly benefitted the government's attempts to apprehend the constructors of the gallows, who clearly had premeditated motives for that day, and who could have provided insightful testimony into the events of January 6.

Letters
- 4/11/24 Letter from Barry Loudermilk to Julie Su
    - CCTV Production Request
- 4/11/24 Letter from Barry Loudermilk to Anita Rizek
    - CCTV Production Request
- 7/22/24 Letter from Barry Loudermilk to Thomas Manger
    - Communications Record Production Request
- 9/17/24 Letter from Barry Loudermilk to Colette Peters
    - CCTV Production Request
- 9/17/24 Letter from Barry Loudermilk to Noel Francisco
    - CCTV Production Request
- 9/17/24 Letter from Barry Loudermilk to Pamela Smith
    - Camera Footage Production Request
- 9/18/24 Letter from Barry Loudermilk to Angela Caesar
    - CCTV Production Request
- 10/17/24 Letter from Barry Loudermilk to Thomas Austin
    - Gallows Information Inquiry
- 10/17/24 Letter from Barry Loudermilk to Colette Peters
    - CCTV Collection Inquiry

United States Secret Service

After the July 2024 assassination attempt on President Trump, the Subcommittee learned that the Department of Homeland Security's Office of Inspector General ("DHS OIG") had two outstanding reports concerning the Department of Homeland Security's ("DHS") response on January 6. One of these outstanding reports was about the Secret Service's preparedness and response concerning President Trump, Vice President Pence, and Vice President-elect Harris. In each of these situations, the Secret Service failed to effectively ensure the safety of their protectees. The failures of the Secret Service on January 6 are directly related to the failures of the Secret Service on July 13, 2024, when President Trump was nearly assassinated in Butler, Pennsylvania.

The Subcommittee worked with the DHS OIG after we became aware that Secretary Mayorkas was delaying the release of the report, *United States Secret Service Preparation for and Response to the Events of January 6, 2021* ("OIG-24-42"), which was released to Congress on August 1, 2024, and to the American public on August 2, 2024. The Subcommittee has seen evidence from the DHS OIG that this report was given to DHS for technical correction and managerial comment on April 30, 2024. However, DHS claimed in an August 1, 2024, letter that they "completed a final multi-layered, multi-stakeholder review of the entire report in six business days."[393]

The Subcommittee viewed OIG-24-42 in camera. The Subcommittee believes there are acceptable redactions in this report but has serious concerns with other redactions that appear to disguise DHS culpability in the intelligence failures leading up to January 6, failures of the Secret Service to adequately plan for Vice President Pence's evacuation, and failure to adequately sweep the DNC before the arrival of Vice President-elect Harris. The Subcommittee believes that there are parallels between the failures of the Secret Service on January 6 and the failures resulting in the attempted assassination of President Trump on July 13, 2024.

Conclusions based on the OIG-24-42 Report:

1. USCP limited the number of Secret Service agents able to be inside the Capitol with Vice President Pence on January 6. The Counterassault team ("CAT") was outside the building and did not enter when it was breached because they did not know the layout of the Capitol.[394]

---

[393] Letter from Zephranie Buetow to Barry Loudermilk, Chairman, Comm. on H. Admin. Oversight Subcomm., (Aug. 1, 2024) (on file with the Subcommittee).

[394] Report, DEP'T OF HOMELAND SEC. OFF. OF THE INSPECTOR GEN., "United States Secret Service Preparation for and Response to the Events of January 6, 2021 (OIG-24-42)" 33-37 (Aug. 2, 2024).

2. The Secret Service either did not receive or did not heed any intelligence products about the threats to the U.S. Capitol on January 6, including the FBI Norfolk Report and the Postal Inspection Service report.[395]

3. Secret Service Protective Intelligence Division Personnel's March for Trump brief did not include any indications of civil disobedience because posters must explicitly state how they will break laws to be noted in the brief.[396]

4. Secret Service guidance did not include instruction on what exterior areas should be swept by a canine for buildings like the DNC. There are varying accounts of whether the bushes should have been swept or not based on guidance given in manuals and by supervisors.[397]

5. The "Two Technologies Rule" states that some combination of Canine, X-Ray, and Explosive Ordinance Detection ("EOD") should be utilized during any explosive sweep. Only canines were used to sweep the DNC because there were issues requesting and obtaining EOD support.[398]

On July 24, 2024, Chairman Loudermilk sent a letter to Secretary Mayorkas demanding he immediately review and clear OIG-24-42 and expressed that it is unacceptable for DHS to delay or deny the DHS OIG access to conduct investigations and publish their findings to both Congress and the American people.[399] On August 1, 2024, DHS OIG was finally given permission to release OIG-24-42. The DHS OIG has been reporting access issues for years, beginning with their Semiannual Report to Congress in September 2021.[400] These access issues include not providing "read-only" access to databases, claiming that the Privacy Act and the Presidential Records Act prohibited the disclosure of records, and stating that some records needed to be cleared by counsel before being turned over to DHS OIG.

DHS OIG further reported that the Secret Service significantly delayed its access to information, impeding the progress of their review for OIG-24-42. For example, the Secret Service delayed DHS OIG's access to internal emails for seven months. When the Secret Service finally responded, it asked DHS OIG to reduce the scope of its request. The reduced scope is concerning, given that several congressional committees sought all electronic records from the Secret Service and the Secret Service appeared unwilling to comply with its own watchdog's request. Chairman Loudermilk and Senator Chuck Grassley (R-IA) sent multiple letters to

---

[395] *Id.* at 19-20.

[396] *Id.* at 16.

[397] *Id.* at 47-48.

[398] *Id.* at 53-54.

[399] Letter from Barry Loudermilk, Chairman, Comm. on H. Admin. Oversight Subcomm., to Alejandro Mayorkas, Secretary, Dep't of Homeland Security (July 24, 2024) (on file with the Subcommittee).

[400] U.S. DEP'T OF HOMELAND SECURITY OFF. OF INSPECTOR GEN., "Semiannual Report to the Congress" 19 (2021).

Secretary Mayorkas and DHS Inspector General Joseph Cuffari, expressing concern at these continued access issues and requests for documents pertaining to these delays. To date, the Subcommittee has not received meaningful responses from either department.

The DHS OIG, who has repeatedly claimed these access issues are pervasive and significantly hinder the ability of the OIG to conduct audits, inspections, and evaluations, is no longer cooperating with the Subcommittee's requests for information. Secretary Mayorkas has refused to engage with the DHS OIG or congressional committees on this issue, claiming that DHS has addressed these allegations—but refuses to provide such responses by DHS to the Subcommittee. Without full cooperation from the executive branch, the Subcommittee is significantly hindered in conducting oversight of the response to January 6 to ensure such failures and oversights never happen again.

Letters

- 5/16/23 Letter from Barry Loudermilk to Robert Contee
  - Record Production Request
- 4/11/24 Letter from Barry Loudermilk to Pamela Smith
  - Record Production Request
- 5/29/24 Letter from Barry Loudermilk to Pamela Smith
  - Record Production Request
- E6/26/24 Letter from Barry Loudermilk to Kimberly Cheatle
  - Radio Recording Production Request
- 8/28/24 Letter from Barry Loudermilk to Ronald Rowe
  - Radio Recording Production Request
- 8/29/24 Letter from Barry Loudermilk to Jessica Taylor
  - Radio Recording Production Request

- 3/23/23 Chairs Loudermilk and Steil Deliver Opening Remarks at Subcommittee on Oversight Hearing
- 3/29/23 Subcommittee on Oversight Chairman Loudermilk Releases First Flash Report on Review of the January 6th Committee
- 5/16/23 Top Takeaways from House Admin Hearing on U.S. Capitol Police
- 5/16/23 Chairs Steil and Loudermilk Deliver Opening Remarks at U.S. Capitol Police Hearing
- 5/22/23 Loudermilk Requests Info from MPD, NARA Related to January 6th
- 6/8/23 ICYMI: Loudermilk Confirms Plain-Clothes MPD Officers Were at the Capitol on January 6th
- 7/19/23 Oversight Subcommittee Chairman Loudermilk's Opening Remarks at Hearing with U.S. Capitol Police's Inspector General
- 7/20/23 Top Takeaways from Hearing with U.S. Capitol Police Inspector General
- 9/1/23 Oversight Subcommittee Chairman Loudermilk Announces Capitol Security Video Footage Policy
- 9/19/23 Oversight Subcommittee Chairman Loudermilk Opening Remarks at Hearing on January 6th Security Failures
- 9/21/23 Top Takeaways from Oversight Subcommittee Hearing on January 6 Security Failures
- 11/17/23 Subcommittee on Oversight releases USCP Video Public Access Policy
- 1/8/24 Oversight Subcommittee Chairman Barry Loudermilk Instructs Cassidy Hutchinson to Produce all January 6th Related Records
- 1/30/24 Chairman Loudermilk to Review Vital January 6th Witness Testimonies from White House
- 2/23/24 Chairman Barry Loudermilk Releases New Information in the January 6, 2021 Gallows Investigation
- 3/1/24 Committee on House Administration Releases 5,000 More Hours of January 6 Footage
- 3/8/24 Chairman Loudermilk Publishes Never-Before Released Anthony Ornato Transcribed Interview
- 3/11/24 Chairman Loudermilk Releases January 6 Initial Findings Report
- 3/12/24 Chairman Loudermilk Delivers Opening Remarks at January 6 Pipe Bomb Hearing
- 3/21/24 Chairman Loudermilk Publishes White House Transcript of President Trump's Valet on January 6, 2021
- 3/22/24 Chairman Loudermilk Releases Additional January 6, 2021 USCP CCTV footage
- 4/15/24 Chairman Loudermilk Releases January 6 Initial Findings Report Documents
- 4/15/24 Chairman Loudermilk Announces Half of All January 6, 2021 Footage Released
- 4/17/24 Chairman Loudermilk Delivers opening Remarks at D.C. National Guard Whistleblower Hearing

- 5/16/24 Chairman Loudermilk Requests Document Production from Jan. 6 Select Committee "Star Witness" Cassidy Hutchinson
- 5/29/24 Chairman Loudermilk Requests Information from MPD Related to Select Committee's False Claim that Trump Planned to Go to Capitol on January 6, 2021
- 6/4/24 Chairman Loudermilk Requests Alyssa Farah Griffin's Communications with Select Committee's "Star Witness" Cassidy Hutchinson
- 6/6/24 Chairman Loudermilk Calls on Fulton County DA Fani Willis to Disclose Communications with Cassidy Hutchinson
- 6/11/24 Nancy Pelosi Contradicts Her Own Narrative of January 6, HBO Footage Shows
- 6/14/24 Chairman Loudermilk Releases Timeline of D.C. National Guard Deployment on January 6, 2021
- 6/17/24 ICYMI: Chairman Loudermilk Sat with Fox News Digital to Discuss the National Guard Delayed Response on Jan. 6, 2021
- 6/21/24 Chairman Loudermilk Calls on DoD IG to Explain January 6 Report
- 6/26/24 Chairman Loudermilk Files Amicus Brief with SCOTUS in Support of Bannon Application for Emergency Relief
- 7/23/24 Chairman Loudermilk Seeks Answers from Capitol Police on Gallows Investigation
- 7/24/24 "You alone are preventing the DHS IG from releasing this report to Congress:" Chairman Loudermilk Demands Secretary Mayorkas Hand Over Secret Service Report on Jan. 6 Events
- 8/2/24 Top Takeaways from DHS OIG Redacted Report on Secret Service January 6 Failures
- 8/20/24 Chairman Loudermilk, Ranking Member Grassley demand answers from Secretary Mayorkas about interference in DHS OIG investigations
- 8/28/24 NEW: Obtained HBO Footage Shows Pelosi Again Taking Responsibility for Capitol Security on January 6
- 9/5/24 NEW: DoD IG Transcripts Contradict Pentagon January 6 Report, Outline "Optics" Concerns as Reason for DCNG Delay
- 9/20/24 Transcripts Show President Trump's Directives to Pentagon Leadership to "Keep January 6 Safe" Were Deliberately Ignored
- 9/25/24 Loudermilk Highlights DoD IG Report Flaws, Sets the Record Straight on January 6, 2021 National Guard Delay
- 10/15/24 New Texts Reveal Liz Cheney Communicated with Cassidy Hutchinson About Her Select Committee Testimony—without Hutchinson's Attorney's Knowledge—Despite Cheney Knowing it was Unethical
- 10/21/24 Expert Analysis Reveals Hutchinson Not the Author of January 6 Tweet
- 11/21/24 DoD Inspector General Concealed January 6 Evidence

The events of January 6, 2021, were preventable. For nearly four years, Democrats pushed the narrative that President Trump was solely responsible for the riot at the Capitol—spending millions of taxpayer dollars on a politically motivated witch hunt while failing to legitimately examine how United States Capitol Leadership was unable to ensure adequate protection for Members of Congress and thousands of congressional staff. Incredibly, it would take nearly four years for video footage to emerge of Speaker Pelosi—in a rare moment of true leadership— admitting that she was fully responsible for the security failures that day. While Democrats politicized Capitol security and prioritized personal political futures, the Subcommittee's unbiased approach to our investigation produced previously undisclosed evidence that undermines the Select Committee's narrative.

Based on the evidence obtained by this Subcommittee, numerous federal laws were likely broken by Liz Cheney, the former Vice Chair of the January 6 Select Committee, and these violations should be investigated by the Federal Bureau of Investigation. Evidence uncovered by the Subcommittee revealed that former Congresswoman Liz Cheney tampered with at least one witness, Cassidy Hutchinson, by secretly communicating with Hutchinson without Hutchinson's attorney's knowledge. This secret communication with a witness is improper and likely violates 18 U.S.C. 1512. Such action is outside the due functioning of the legislative process and therefore not protected by the Speech and Debate clause.

The Federal Bureau of Investigation must also investigate Representative Cheney for violating 18 U.S.C. 1622, which prohibits any person from procuring another person to commit perjury. Based on the evidence obtained by this Subcommittee, Hutchinson committed perjury when she lied under oath to the Select Committee. Additionally, Hutchinson was interviewed by the FBI as part of its investigation into President Trump. This Subcommittee sought a copy of the FBI report 302, documenting this interview and Hutchinson's statements, but the FBI has refused to produce this vital document. The FBI must immediately review the testimony given by Hutchinson in this interview to determine if she also lied in her FBI interview, and, if so, the role former Representative Cheney played in instigating Hutchinson to radically change her testimony.

The FBI still has not admitted what records it received from the Select Committee. Some statements made by Special Counsel Jack Smith's team revealed that the Special Prosecutor received witness transcripts that were not released publicly by the Select Committee. However, the Special Counsel has never acknowledged how many transcripts he received, or whether he also received the video recordings of these transcribed interviews that the Select Committee failed to archive.

It is clear from Congressman Thompson's admission that he violated House Rules by deleting the Select Committee's recordings of transcribed interviews. The Select Committee recorded hundreds of transcribed interviews, but Representative Thompson chose to delete these recordings instead of archiving them as required by House Rules. As Chair of the Select Committee, Representative Thompson was solely responsible for complying with House Rules related to the archiving of committee records such as these recordings. By deleting these recordings, Representative Thompson prevented House Republicans from reviewing these videos which could have contained important information, specifically with respect to the interviews of Cassidy Hutchinson.

These crimes must be fully investigated and individuals held responsible to maintain the trust of the American People in their government.

NATIONAL GUARD TIMELINE
PRIOR TO JANUARY 6, 2021

12/31/20

D.C. Mayor Muriel Bowser requests Secretary of the Army Ryan McCarthy provide D.C. National Guard (DCNG) on January 5-6 to support Metro Police Department.

1/3/21

Acting Secretary of Defense, Chris Miller, meets with President Trump at the White House; POTUS concurs that Secretary Miller activate DCNG to support law enforcement.

1/3/21

U.S. Capitol Police ("USCP") Chief Steven Sund asks Senate Sergeant at Arms ("SSAA") Michael Stenger and House Sergeant at Arms ("HSAA") Paul Irving for authority to have DCNG assist with security on January 6, 2021.

Both SSAA and HSAA deny Chief Sund's request.

1/3/21

USCP Chief Sund advises DCNG Major General (MG) William Walker that USCP may need DCNG support on January 6 but **does not have the Capitol Police Board authorization to request at this time** because SSAA and HSAA have denied the request.

1/4/21

Secretary Miller and Secretary McCarthy formally approve D.C. Mayor Bowser's December 31 request for DCNG to support with Traffic Control Points ("TCPs").

1/4/21

On a call with Mayor Bowser, White House Chief of Staff Mark Meadows offers 10,000 DCNG to support public safety.

1/5/21

USCP Chief Sund informs SSAA and HSAA in separate discussions about the DCNG's ability to provide troops if **authorization is granted.**

1/5/21

Mayor Bowser sends letter to the Department of Defense (DoD) confirming the City of D.C. is not requesting support from additional law enforcement and discourages any additional deployment.

1/5/21

President Trump calls Secretary Miller and offers 10,000 troops to maintain public safety on January 6, 2021.

NATIONAL GUARD TIMELINE

ON JANUARY 6, 2021

HOUSE ADMINISTRATION
SUBCOMMITTEE ON
OVERSIGHT

11:35 AM

Demonstrators start to
move from the Ellipse to
the US Capitol.

12:53 PM

First breach of USCP's
outer perimeter on the
West Front of the US
Capitol.

1:40 PM

HSAA Irving seeks out
Speaker Pelosi's Chief of
Staff, Terri McCullough, on
the House Floor to relay
Chief Sund's request for
National Guard support to
the Speaker.

1:49 PM

Chief Sund calls MG Walker
and asks for immediate
National Guard assistance,
stating that the security
perimeter at the U.S. Capitol
has been breached.

2:08 PM

Chief Sund calls HSAA
Irving and is informed
that the Capitol Police
Board has formally
approved the request
for DCNG.

2:10 PM

Chief Sund calls MG Walker
requesting immediate support
from DCNG. MG Walker advises
Sund that the DCNG Quick
Reaction Force could be ready
to deploy immediately if
authorized.

**Secretary McCarthy withholds
unilateral approval to deploy
the QRF.**

2:12 PM

First breach of the Capitol
Building.

2:19 PM

MG Walker emails Secretary
McCarthy advising of Chief
Sund's request for
immediate assistance.

Receives no email or phone
response.

2:30 PM

Secretary McCarthy is not
present on the 2:30 call.

Secretary McCarthy meets
with Secretary Miller at the
Pentagon to discuss
requests for immediate
DCNG deployment. .

2:30-2:55 PM

Dr. Christopher Rodriguez (DCHSEMA)
establishes conference call with DC
and Military leaders to seek Secretary
of the Army's authorization for
immediate deployment of DCNG.

Multiple participants recall **LTG Piatt
and LTG Flynn state they don't like the
"optics of the National Guard standing
in a line with the Capitol in the
background" and their best military
advice would be to recommend that
Secretary McCarthy not support the
request.**

2:44 PM

Shots fired inside
the US Capitol
Building.

2:50 PM

Members in the House Gallery
evacuate.

3:04 PM

**Secretary Miller provides verbal
approval to Secretary McCarthy**
for the immediate mobilization,
activation, and deployment of the
DCNG to the U.S. Capitol,
including the deployment of a
Quick Reaction Force.

3:05 PM
Secure Video Teleconference ('SVTC') initiated between DCNG and Secretary McCarthy's senior leadership.

3:05 PM
Secretary McCarthy provides update to Speaker Pelosi and Senator Schumer regarding his 3:04pm conversation with Secretary Miller.

3:19 PM
Secretary McCarthy calls Senator Schumer and Speaker Pelosi again, explaining that Secretary Miller has indeed approved immediate DCNG mobilization.

3:26 PM
Secretary McCarthy calls Mayor Bowser and MPD Chief Contee to tell them there has been no denial of their request and conveys Secretary Miller's approval of the immediate activation of DCNG.

3:26 PM
Chief Sund calls MG Walker requesting immediate assistance.

MG Walker informs Sund DCNG deployment authorization has not been communicated by Secretary McCarthy.

3:46 PM
Chief Sund again calls MG Walker requesting immediate assistance.

MG Walker reiterates he has not received deployment approval from Secretary McCarthy.

3:48 PM
Secretary McCarthy leaves the Pentagon for MPD HQ to meet with Mayor Bowser and MPD Chief Contee to develop an Operational Plan (OPLAN).

Secretary McCarthy stops at FBI HQ along the way.

4:22 PM
Chief Sund again calls MG Walker requesting immediate assistance.

MG Walker emphasizes he has not received deployment approval.

4:30 PM
Secretary McCarthy calls Secretary Miller again to brief him on the OPLAN.

Neither DCNG nor USCP are involved in the development of this OPLAN.

4:35 PM
Fatality inside US Capitol Building.

4:47 PM
Secretary McCarthy participates in national news press conference with Mayor Bowser stating that the DCNG has been mobilized – despite approval not yet communicated to MG Walker.

5:08 PM
MG Walker receives order via SVTC to deploy DCNG from Secretary McCarthy's Chief of Staff, General McConville, in passing.

5:08 PM
First DCNG bus departs DC Armory.

5:20 PM
DCNG arrive at the USCP HQ to be sworn in by USCP.

5:55 PM
DCNG Guardsmen arrive at US Capitol.

Architect of the Capitol
U.S. Capitol, Room SB-16
Washington, DC 20515
202.228.1793

www.aoc.gov

October 28, 2024

The Honorable Barry Loudermilk
Chairman
Subcommittee on Oversight
Committee on House Administration
U.S. House of Representatives
Washington, DC 20515

Dear Mr. Chairman:

Thank you for your letter dated October 17, 2024. Please see the responses to your inquiry below.

Question 1: A list of all employees involved in dismantling and transporting the gallows on and after January 7, 2021.

Response 1: Former Architect Brett Blanton directed/oversaw the cleanup of the U.S. Capitol Grounds after January 6, 2021. No records were kept for other individuals directly involved in specific aspects of the clean up effort.

Question 2: A detailed account of what happened to the gallows materials after entering the lot at the above location on and after January 7, 2021.

Response 2: Gallows material was collected with other damaged property, trash and debris. The gallows consisted of a platform and wooden "upright." The upright was removed from the platform in order to place it in a truck. Architect of the Capitol (AOC) employees removed other debris and damaged property, including an Olmsted light fixture. The truck returned to 14 E Street, SE, and the damaged Olmsted light fixture was removed from the truck and saved for restoration. The gallows material and other trash and debris were then transported to a waste management facility for disposal.

Question 3: What or who initiated AOC's response to the gallows on the morning of January 7, 2021?

Response 3: As part of the AOC's mission, the agency has the responsibility to serve Congress and preserve our facilities and grounds. The mission priority on January 7, 2021, and in the following weeks, was to safely and efficiently restore the grounds and prepare for the Presidential Inauguration. The AOC organized jurisdictional staff and began clean-up and restoration efforts of the U.S. Capitol Grounds, including Union Square and the gallows.

Question 4: Since AOC took possession of the gallows, has any federal agency or congressional committee contacted AOC to either inspect or inquire into the whereabout of the gallows? If so, please provide a list of the date and requesting entity, as well as AOC's response.

Response 4: The AOC is not aware of any other agency or committee that has specifically inquired about the gallows.

Sincerely,

Thomas E. Austin, PE, CCM, PMP
Architect of the Capitol

Doc. No. 241025-00-01

Innovative Driven, Inc.
1700 North Moore Street
Suite 1500
Arlington, VA 22209
www.innovativedriven.com

To: National Archives and Records Administration

From: John J. Cain, Senior Litigation Support Consultant

Date: December 28, 2022

Re: Archive of the January 6th Committee's Relativity database

I. Overview

What was provided to NARA as "J6C_Archive" is a selected export of the main "Productions" database (called a "workspace" in Relativity) in the committee's Relativity environment. Relativity[1] is web-based electronic discovery[2] software that is used to house, search, and code large numbers of electronic documents for litigation and investigatory purposes.

The "Productions" workspace was a depository of many of the documents produced to the committee by government agencies, Trump administration officials, subpoenaed third parties, interested third parties, and others. It also contained transcripts and exhibits for the depositions and interviews conducted by the committee, as well as research done by the committee and outside experts.

Committee work-product was excluded from the export, as were selected documents the committee deemed as sensitive. However, objective coding done for organizational purposes (e.g. the producing party, the date of production, etc.) was included.

What follows are descriptions of the primary aspects of the "J6C_Archive" export that will need to be understood when this is imported into a database software in the future.

II. Loadfiles

Two loadfiles were included in the export: a delimited data file and an image loadfile. These both are standard deliverables in the electronic discovery industry and can be imported into most database software.

The Concordance data file (DAT) contains metadata and objective coding fields, as well as links to the native and text associated with a document. This is a flat delimited file, meaning that while the fields are organized into columns (like Excel),

---

[1] https://www.relativity.com/. The committee had their own Relativity environment separate from other Innovative Driven clients. The software version used was 11.1.582.3.
[2] https://en.wikipedia.org/wiki/Electronic_discovery

Innovative Driven, Inc.

1700 North Moore Street
Suite 1500
Arlington, VA 22209
www.innovativedriven.com

the entire file is only plain text and the columns are represented by special characters. These characters are:

Value	Character	ASCII Number
Column	¶	020
Quote	þ	254
Newline	®	174
Multi-Value	;	059
Nested Value	\	092

The break between columns is usually going to be represented by þ¶þ.

Each row is a new document (record). There is a link to the native file in the "FILE_PATH" field and a link to the text file in the "Text Precedence" field. These are relative links, and you need to adjust these links depending on where the data resides on your server.

The Opticon loadfile (OPT) contains relative paths to image files (either TIFF or JPG format) associated with documents. Not all documents have images, only documents that Innovative Driven created images for or were produced to the committee as images.

Each line in the OPT is a page (instead of a document like the DAT), and the lines are in the following format:

[page identifier],[volume],[path to images file]\[image file name],[document break indicator]

The document break indicator will either be Y,,,[page count] for a new document or ,,, for a page that isn't a new document.

Like the DAT file, you will need to update the relative link in the OPT depending on where the data resides on your network.

Innovative Driven, Inc.

1700 North Moore Street
Suite 1500
Arlington, VA 22209
www.innovativedriven.com

III. Identifiers

The unique identifier field in the export is the DOCID field; every document has a DOCID value. If a document is stamped with them, bates numbers[3] are captured in the BEGBATES and ENDBATES fields. Not all documents have bates numbers.

This is what any particular DOCID value means:

CTRL[10 digits] – this was processed by Innovative Driven, because it was produced to the committee as a native file or a PDF.

CTRL[10 digits].[4 digits] – this was also processed by Innovative Driven, but it's a child document to the DOCID value before the period. See "Relationships" below.

CTRL[10 digits]_[5 digits] – this document is the product of re-unitization, meaning that the original document (the DOCID before the underscore) was divided into multiple documents. This was done usually when a production was provided as a large PDF with no document breaks. The document breaks were created by looking at the document and manually assigning them. The version of the document before re-unitization was not provided in the export.

DOCID = BEGBATES – this document was provided as part of a load file formatted production (like the export the committee provided to NARA).

DOCID begins with REL or USSS – this documents was initially imported into another Relativity workspace in the committee's environment before being migrated to the Productions workspace.

IV. Relationships

In electronic discovery terminology, a "family" is a group of documents that are associated with one another, with one document being primary (the "parent") and the rest being secondary (the "children"). Most often this refers to an email (parent) and its attachments (children), but it can also refer to a container file and its contents. In the export this also refers to a transcript and its exhibits.

All documents in a family share a value in the DOCBEGATT field. This value is the DOCID of the parent document. Only children will have the DOCPARENTID field populated, also with the value of the parent's DOCID.

Forensic duplicates will all share a value in the MD5Hash field.

---

[3] https://en.wikipedia.org/wiki/Bates_numbering

Innovative Driven, Inc.

1700 North Moore Street
Suite 1500
Arlington, VA 22209
www.innovativedriven.com

V.   Notes on Metadata

The availability of metadata for documents in the export was dependent on the metadata provided by the producing parties and the format of each production. If a production was native files, then Innovative Driven could extract that metadata during processing. If a production was in load file format, then metadata was provided and loaded, although limited to the fields the party produced. Both of these formats usually resulted in sufficient metadata.

If a production was provided as PDFs (as many were), then limited metadata was available. For instance, if emails were converted to PDF and produced to the committee as such, only the metadata of the PDF would be available, none of the email metadata (From, To, DateSent, MailSubject, etc.) would be retained.

Made in the USA
Las Vegas, NV
22 December 2024

15237638R00070